Finite, Contingent, and Free

Finite, Contingent, and Free

A New Ethics of Acceptance

Joyce Kloc McClure

ROWMAN & LITTLEFIELD PUBLISHERS, INC.
Lanham • Boulder • New York • Oxford

ROWMAN & LITTLEFIELD PUBLISHERS, INC.

Published in the United States of America
by Rowman & Littlefield Publishers, Inc.
A Member of the Rowman & Littlefield Publishing Group
4501 Forbes Boulevard, Suite 200, Lanham, Maryland 20706
www.rowmanlittlefield.com

PO Box 317
Oxford
OX2 9RU, UK

British Library Cataloguing in Publication Information Available

Library of Congress Cataloging-in-Publication Data

McClure, Joyce Kloc, 1955–
  Finite, contingent, and free : a new ethics of acceptance / Joyce Kloc
McClure.
      p. cm.
Includes bibliographical references and index.
    ISBN 0-7425-1404-8 (alk. paper) — ISBN 0-7425-1405-6 (pbk. : alk.
paper)
  1. Ethics. 2. Social acceptance. I. Title.
BJ1012 .M316 2003
171' .3—dc21   2002152680

Printed in the United States of America

∞™ The paper used in this publication meets the minimum requirements of
American National Standard for Information Sciences—Permanence of Paper for
Printed Library Materials, ANSI/NISO Z39.48-1992.

To my children,
Mary and Joe Kloc,
with love and gratitude for all that you are.

Contents

Acknowledgments

After writing a book that attempts to deal with our deep dependencies in life, I would like to acknowledge some of the people upon whom the completion of this book depends. My first and most specific debt is to Margaret Farley. Only Margaret could know the extent of my debt to her as teacher, advisor, and friend. This book grew out of my dissertation at Yale, and I have her as well as Gene Outka and Richard Fern to thank for the many ways they helped me shape this project from its inception, and Tom Ogletree to thank for his helpful comments on it.

I would also like to express my gratitude to my colleagues in the Religion Department at Oberlin College. I couldn't wish for a more supportive and challenging environment. Thanks to James Dobbins and Paula Richman, who had the knack for offering key advice at just the right times. David Kamitsuka read all of the manuscript; some parts more than once. It was enormously helpful to have the insights of such a fine mind as his. I especially appreciate his generosity in helping me develop my arguments regarding Rahner and Rorty. I am grateful to Oberlin College for the B. Wade and Jane B. White Fellowship in the Humanities which enabled me to complete a full draft of this manuscript.

I benefited greatly from the wisdom and patience of the editors at Rowman & Littlefield. Jim Langford offered encouragement and concise suggestions that propelled me to think a number of matters through more thoroughly as I progressed with the book. Jason Proetorius guided the book through the editorial phases, as did John Wehmueller early on. Dave Compton served as copyeditor. Everyone at Rowman & Littlefield was helpful and kind, attributes I appreciated greatly.

For remarkably precise and clear proofreading, I would like to thank Maria Esguerra and Zeeba Daruwalla. Zeeba also assisted with the compilation of the index.

The process of writing a book and preparing it for publication is long and demanding. Keeping up one's spirit throughout can be challenging, and I am grateful to those who helped me do this. My sister, Rosaly Piro, was always there for me, and as always, I am thankful for her presence in my life. I am grateful to Vicki Hoffer, Vicki Hutlock, and Sue McBride for continuing our long and sustaining friendships and to Wendy Kozol for cheering me on whenever I needed it most. For his support as I conclude this process, I am grateful to Emil Babyak.

Finally, I would like to acknowledge a number of people whose deaths forced me to confront the finitude and contingency of existence. These people enriched my own life in immeasurable ways, and their deaths drove me deeper into questions about the conditions of our existence and their possible meanings for our lives. They are Rosemary and Raymond Walczak, Nancy LaFrance, Linda Blomquist, Anna Lamberti, Page Romer, and E. Mark Kloc Jr.

Joyce Kloc McClure
Oberlin College

Introduction

$\mathcal{A}$t the center of ethical inquiry is the human person.[1] Ethical theory concerns what human persons should do, how they should develop, and what they should seek to bring about. Yet a sensitive consideration of the diversity of human experiences tells us that not all human persons have the same potentialities and abilities to do what is 'right', grow as they would wish, and live a 'good' life. Each individual person has specific limitations and dependencies that restrict and shape the kinds of choices that will be made and the kind of life that will be lived. What human persons share, however, is a common vulnerability to finitude, understood as limitation, and contingency, understood as dependency, which, as conditions of existence, profoundly affect the lives we lead. We all live, then, as finite and contingent beings.

A sensitive consideration of the diversity of human experiences also tells us that making ethical choices in the course of life is often perplexing and sometimes overwhelmingly difficult for persons. Jeremy Bentham had a remarkable optimism about the ability of utilitarianism to guide each person through the choices of her or his life. He believed that this ethical theory could be encapsulated in a pamphlet that could be consulted easily whenever an ethical choice needed to be made.[2] Bentham's dream has never come true. Although some individuals possess great confidence in their own ability to lead the blameless life, most of us struggle to discern how we should live. We may feel ourselves obligated to others, yet we are unsure how to live out the requirements of obligation. We may understand ourselves also to be obligated to our own selves, yet here again, we are unsure as to what the obligation entails. Christians have a particular conception of their obligation to others, known generally as neighbor love, yet are often at a loss to determine the extent of the obligation, the place to strike a balance between the need of the neighbor and the limits of the self. Moreover, as we wrestle with these difficulties, we know that they are complicated by our awareness that not everyone has the same capacities, not everyone has the same degree of need, and not everyone has even the same kinds of challenges in life. This means that the place of balance we seek to find between the needs of the other and the limits of the self will vary, depending on who our neighbor is and our assessment of our own capabilities.

The situation is further complicated by the fact that while we perceive ourselves as making ethical choices, this very perception entails an assumption that we have the capacity to make choices of any kind. It assumes, in other words, that human persons are not only finite and contingent but also free. This assumption, however, has been contested vigorously since the eighteenth century, largely on the basis of the acceptance of mechanistic determinism as the overarching theoretical paradigm for describing cause and effect in the physical world.[3] Attempts to account for freedom without challenging this paradigm have met consistently with criticism and rejection. But if ethical theory is to have its proper weight, it must have a way of accounting for human choice. Given the sea change in scientific thought on this matter in the twentieth century, there is theoretical room now to consider human persons as possessing a capacity for genuine freedom in making ethical choices.

Yet even if human persons are accepted as finite, contingent, and free, the question still remains, How free? This is a crucial question, because freedom, to the extent that it exists, gives human persons the capacity to transcend both their limitation, that is, their finitude, and their dependency on factors outside themselves, that is, their contingency. If the recognition of finitude and contingency points to the vulnerability of human persons, the possibility of freedom suggests that this vulnerability is not total. Ethicists and philosophers have focused their examination of the degree of this vulnerability under the topic of moral luck. The entire moral luck debate, however, has been conducted under the same assumption of mechanistic determinism in the physical world that has limited the consideration of human freedom. To come closer to an understanding of the depth of human vulnerability to the conditions of existence, the question of moral luck must be taken up anew, this time under the new scientific paradigm that challenges the assumption of mechanistic determinism. What comes of this analysis is not only a greater appreciation of the depth of human vulnerability, but also an indication that ethical inquiry needs to be pointed in a new direction, toward active acceptance rather than assessment of moral responsibility, or moral judgment of actions. Emphasis on the assignment of moral responsibility is closely allied with the determination of causes that so characterize science in the mechanistic view. The shift in world view, then, suggests the need for a shift in direction for ethical theory. A new ethics of acceptance is identified at the end of the third chapter as a way to make that shift.

A new understanding of the human person as finite, contingent, and free emerges from these considerations. Thus, the first part of this project is theoretical, divided into three chapters that address, first, the human person as finite and contingent; second, the human person as free; and third, the degree of vulnerability of the human person. Part I generates a view of the human person that is consistent with a fundamental assertion of the New Testament: that human persons are deeply vulnerable to the conditions of their existence, but that even this vulnerability has a limit. The Christian affirmation of the salvific work of Christ, securing a measure of invulnerability to the world, and to finitude in particular, is wholly in line with the view generated here. Although the emphasis here is on the significance of this view for ethical theory, it is important to see that it is entirely consistent with Christianity's basic understanding of the possible limits to human vulnerability. In the final chapter of the book, the religious significance of this view will be addressed explicitly.

The second part of this project concerns practice and has the goal of coming to understand fully the implications of this view of the human person for ethical discernment and obligations in order to develop a new approach to ethics. If the basic work of the first part is to get a clearer picture of just what it is to be human in terms of the fundamental conditions and capacities of human existence, then the work of the second part is to answer the question, What does this mean for living an ethical life? To begin to see the complexity of the proper moral response in the face of contingent and finite existence, an ethical analysis of Charles Dickens's *Our Mutual Friend* is undertaken in chapter 4, because it offers the opportunity to see both human vulnerability to the conditions of existence and the task of active acceptance presented in the concrete terms of human lives, rather than in the abstractions of philosophical discourse. In this novel, Dickens engages the questions at hand directly and consistently in the lives of the characters that people the novel's world, thereby providing us with knowledge specifically about what it is to *live* as finite and contingent beings.[4]

Our Mutual Friend serves as a rich resource for this analysis for two reasons. First, it is recognized as a deeply existential novel; no new claim is being made here that Dickens self-consciously addresses existential questions.[5] As such, it engages the very topic of interest here. Second, in this novel

Dickens offers his mature ethical insight into both human vulnerability and the task of self-acceptance. Dickens's entire corpus is widely recognized for its social critique. Throughout his literary career, Dickens displayed a deep commitment to social ethics. Hardly an English reader exists even today who is unaware of his concern for the conditions of the poor in nineteenth-century London. But Dickens also engaged more theoretical questions of ethics consistently throughout his writing. Questions of moral responsibility, character, and even ethical theory appear again and again in his novels. This deep and life-long commitment to moral questions makes his last complete novel a particularly rich source for ethical reflection. Moreover, although Dickens did not write explicitly as a Christian ethicist, his corpus shows a deep commitment to Christian virtues as important to life.[6] His examination of human vulnerability, then, is considered as a source of wisdom from a thoughtful Christian perspective on both the conditions of existence and the implications of them for our lives.

This novel provides a bridge to the normative end of this project for, in addition to exploring how vulnerable human beings are to the conditions of their existence, it asks the normative question, How are human beings to act in this world, given the fundamental conditions of their existence? Dickens considers the issue in terms of identity and, in his multifaceted treatment, shows us again and again the necessity of genuine self-acceptance as a fundamental ethical task. In a world where we are deeply vulnerable to our past, to the people in our lives, and to what happens to us, our self-acceptance, understood as extending to include all of these factors as well as our own true selves, must precede our efforts to help others and ourselves if our actions are to be effective. Dickens helps us to expand our understanding of the task of acceptance identified at the end of chapter 3 and to more fully develop that understanding in chapter 5.

That active acceptance should emerge as the proper response to the conditions of human existence also fits well with Christian theological understanding of the need for acceptance of self before God. What is new here is the ethical focus as well as the way this acceptance is articulated in terms of the fundamental conditions of existence. It is possible only because of the human capacity for freedom, but it is also limited and shaped by human vulnerability to the conditions of existence. In the final chapter, the idea that active acceptance of one's finitude and contingency is required for effective moral action is expanded beyond its pragmatic content to an understanding of this self-acceptance and, by logical extension, the acceptance of the finitude and contingency of others, as an obligation. This acceptance has both a religious and an ethical dimension that must be explored together to understand how active acceptance is both a religious and an ethical obligation. Once the obligatory nature of active acceptance is established, then the way in which active acceptance helps us identify when we have a further obligation to ourselves or others, and what that obligation entails, is examined. Thus, in part II a new methodology for discerning appropriate moral action is developed based on the understanding of the human person established in part I: as finite, contingent, and free. This new methodology constitutes an ethics of acceptance.

This book seeks, then, to develop a new approach to ethics that is grounded in our experience as finite, contingent, and free and is consonant with a Christian understanding of what it is to be human and to be obligated to ourselves and others. A few words on the book's methodology are in order. The turn to finitude and contingency as fundamental conditions of existence, as well as the focus on the issue of human freedom, are features that reflect the author's commitment to approach ethics from what is best described as a Roman Catholic point of view. That is to say, it is deeply informed by Roman Catholicism's embrace of turning to nature and reason to make its case, from a perspective that is profoundly and foundationally shaped by the Christian story as told in the New Testament and by the Christian hope for humankind and redemption more generally. As such, it is a project that is meant to be open and persuasive to Christians and non-Christians alike, although the articulation of religious acceptance in the final chapter will of course resonate more with Christians.

But more is at stake than a specific point of view, however important that may be. The methodology itself was also chosen to help make progress beyond three perplexing difficulties for theologians and philosophers today, including the religious ethicist. The first is the problem of justifying any type of claim about what it is to be a human being that does not violate the particularity of each human being. Compounding this has been a problem especially relevant to the ethicist: the difficulty of making a case for the existence of human freedom, where the entire discipline in some way engages or depends on the need for human beings to make choices, and evaluate their choices, in the context of their lives. The long-standing and all-dominating view of the world as it is leaves little room for a theoretical grounding of freedom, and so philosophers and theologians alike have taken a variety of tacks to try to assume, evade, make compatible, or soften the significance of human freedom vis-à-vis determinism.

The description of finitude and contingency in the first chapter seeks to address the first problem, that of saying something about what it is to be human that is universally true to a practical extent without violating particularity.

The description in chapter 1 identifies finitude and contingency as conditions that are fundamental for human existence and therefore common to all, but since it is our finitude and contingency that give rise to our particularity, these conditions of existence seem good candidates for articulating what is universal while respecting what is particular.

The second problem is taken up in light of the answer to the first. That is, the very fact that our finitude and contingency create particular lives, lives that encounter particular choices, requires that the question of freedom be addressed. Because chapter 2 offers a new, more scientifically sound account than mechanistic determinism as an overarching view with room for freedom—a view, moreover, that also gains support from the very considerations of finitude and contingency explored in chapter 1—we may begin to think again about human persons as substantively free in a real sense. This means that we no longer need to restrict ourselves, theoretically at least, to thinking of human persons only 'as if' they were free, or to constructing models for considering freedom in nonsubstantive ways. Yet if this makes it possible to speak of human persons as possessing some degree of freedom, it does so with the implication that freedom is had in a context where finitude and contingency profoundly shape our lives. This approach also recognizes that it is not possible to speak of human persons as free in an absolute sense. Freedom, to the extent that it exists, can be only a matter of degree.

Making some progress on these two fronts, however, could leave us with a third problem, one common to an endeavor of this kind: abstraction. Having worked on the topics of finitude, contingency, and freedom for some time, the author is keenly aware of how easily abstract wanderings can bedevil such considerations. However, the methodology that risks creating this problem is also its antidote. Finitude and contingency are taken up precisely because these are features of concrete existence, and the issue of freedom must then be considered because it arises directly in relation to them. These features literally confront us as we live. Moreover, the decision to turn to literary analysis from an ethical point of view reflects not just a turn to a source of deep reflection and a presentation of experience, but also a commitment to keep the ethical analysis grounded, that is, consonant with the conditions of particular lives, the conditions under which all ethical action occurs.

This book seeks to move beyond the three problems noted above and clear the way for the development of a fruitful new approach that is philosophically sound, consistent with key Christian understandings, and productive of a concrete ethics that arises from a conception of the human person as finite, contingent, and free. The final chapter offers a specific approach to ethics that can assist us in understanding morality anew and in discerning how we are to act if we are indeed finite, contingent, and free. Admittedly, seeking to develop a way of understanding that avoids the three problems noted above and generates a new approach to ethics is an ambitious agenda. But the book is intended as a beginning, as a new way of asking questions about ethics, not as the answer to the ongoing ethical questions that life poses for us.

Notes

1. Though ethical theories may place God, or the whole of the universe, at their center, all of them nonetheless must address the human person in a central way.

2. Alan Ryan, "Introduction," in *Utilitarianism and Other Essays: J. S. Mill and Jeremy Bentham*, ed. Alan Ryan (New York: Penguin, 1987), 29.

3. Prior to this time, the central debate in Christianity about human freedom focused on whether or not humans have freedom vis-à-vis God's will.

4. As Martha C. Nussbaum puts it, "Literary form is not separable from philosophical content, but is, itself, a part of content—an integral part, then, of the search for and the statement of truth." Nussbaum, *Love's Knowledge: Essays on Philosophy and Literature* (New York: Oxford University Press, 1990), 3. She goes on to argue that novels have an epistemological value that adds to the academic philosophical enterprise. She asserts, "To bring novels into moral philosophy is not . . . to bring them to some academic discipline which happens to ask ethical questions. It is to bring them into connection with our deepest practical searching, for ourselves and others, the searching in connection with which the influential philosophical conceptions of the ethical were originally developed, . . ." the search for an answer to the question, "'How Should One Live?'" (23–24).

5. See Joseph Gold, *Charles Dickens: Radical Moralist* (Minneapolis: University of Minnesota Press, 1972), 5–6.

6. For example, in *Hard Times*, Dickens's critique of utilitarianism, Thomas Gradgrind is so transformed from his hardness in wanting only the facts that by the end of the novel the reader is given a peek at his future, in which, Dickens suggests, he bends "his hitherto inflexible theories to appointed circumstances, making his facts and figures subservient to Faith, Hope, and Charity." Dickens, *Hard Times* (New York: Harper and Row, 1965), chapter 9. Also, Dennis Walder notes that, according to John Forster, "Dickens was unswervingly faithful to Christianity and the Church on 'essential points.'" See Walder, *Dickens and Religion* (Boston: Allen & Unwin, 1981), 15. Walder references Forster, *The Life of Charles Dickens*, ed. J. W. T. Ley (London: Cecil Palmer, 1928), 818–20.

The Human Person
and the Terms of Existence

CHAPTER ONE

Contingency and Finitude as Conditions of Existence

$\mathcal{U}$nless we are masters of denial, we all at some point in our lives experience our vulnerability, the fact that we can be affected by what happens to us.[1] It may be that a particular event, such as the death of a parent or grandparent, brings the fact of our vulnerability home to us. When someone close to us dies, we are forced to face the vulnerability of physical existence, but not just that. We must also face the fact that the part of our lives that we shared with that person could be lived in memory but no longer in fact. One can no longer talk about life over a cup of tea with one's mother after she dies. Or, we may be made to face our vulnerability by an experience of romantic love, in which we feel our hope and joy so wrapped up in the life of another person that we realize how deeply we depend on others for the things that matter to us. Part of yielding to another in love is coming to trust that our vulnerability will be respected. Even the experience of having to make significant life choices highlights our vulnerability. We cannot know if we are making the "best" choice for ourselves and those we care about, yet we know that much depends on the future ramifications of the choice made. When we feel anxious and uncertain about a particular decision, such as whether to accept a new position of employment or stay in our present one, we are experiencing our vulnerability to the outcomes of our choices.

Whatever the experiences that bring our vulnerability into focus so that we are keenly aware of it, they are only part of the story. It is also the case that vulnerability pervades our lives in far less obvious ways. The myriad indicators of our vulnerability may not break through to explicit awareness, but they remain in the fabric of our lives. What is needed is a clearer picture of this vulnerability to the conditions of our existence, because it is as vulnerable beings that we live, making choices and in the process trying to meet our obligations to ourselves and one another. The first task here, then, is to look at these conditions of existence to and through which we are vulnerable: contingency and finitude.

The purpose of this chapter is to provide a description of finitude and contingency as fundamental conditions of existence, as the first step in exploring their ethical implications. Fundamental conditions of existence are modes of being without which we would not exist, at least not in any recognizable way. Our very existence is conditional on them because it is made possible by them. It is of note that finitude and contingency are being considered as fundamental but not necessarily the only fundamental conditions of existence. Given the limitations of our ability to conceptualize and articulate existence and experience, it is unlikely that we could ever claim to have a communicable grasp on human existence itself. Moreover, there may well be other conditions or features of existence that are equally as fundamental as finitude and contingency but genuinely distinct from them. Finally, there may be other features of existence that either involve finitude and/or contingency or for which we must employ the concepts of finitude and/or contingency in our attempt to articulate them, and yet are not merely reducible to finitude and contingency. Paul Ricouer's concept of fallibility comes to mind as a possible example of this type.[2]

Such disclaimers notwithstanding, the claim is being made here that finitude and contingency are genuinely fundamental to human existence. Ultimately, because these conditions are fundamental, obtaining at all levels of existence, what can be described is our experience of them, in an effort to get at how we ought to live in those conditions. They are not conditions or features that we merely encounter in the course of our existence; instead, they are conditions in which and through which we exist. Reaching the goal of developing a description of our experience of them, then, involves getting at what is essential in our experience of these fundamental conditions.

A complicating factor in this endeavor is that we experience the conditions of our existence as an existential whole. However, this existential whole is not a conceptual whole. The human mind, complex as it is, needs to focus its attention in order to understand such a complex reality. Therefore, prior to describing the experience of contingency and finitude together, we need a description of the experience of each condition. Three descriptions are therefore required: descriptions of the experience of finitude, of contingency, and of finitude and contingency together. Unfortunately, since the first two descriptions are of conditions abstracted from their actual dynamic interrelation, they appear somewhat detached from the complexity of life. It is important to bear in mind that the descriptions do refer, however abstractly, to features that affect us in concrete and often painful ways. Our finitude and contingency profoundly shape our lives, to the point of carving out for us our most basic struggles.[3] It is not until we get to the description of the experience of contingency and finitude, however, that due attention can be given to the struggle and challenge of the experience of being both contingent and finite beings.

Before turning to the descriptions, a word on methodology is in order. Two points require elucidation. The first concerns what is involved in the descriptive effort. Developing meaningful descriptions that will aid in further philosophical reflection is a three-part task. Immediate focus, conceptual analysis, and clear rendering of the experience are all important facets of the task. By immediate focus I mean that specific attention must be paid to lived experience, as it occurs. In the case at hand, attention must be paid to aspects of life that suggest finitude, for example. These immediate events must also to some degree be analyzed. We must examine the concepts implied by or underlying the events in order to understand the significance of the experience under focus. Part of this analytic step involves looking at what others have had to say that bears on the aspect of existence being described. Therefore, each of these descriptions draws on theological, philosophical, and psychological sources where appropriate. However, the present task, that of developing descriptions of the experiences of finitude, of contingency, and of finitude and contingency together for moral wisdom and ultimately a new approach to ethics, is original and largely constructive.[4] Finally, a clear rendering, a description, must result that is more than a record of "raw" experience, for what is wanted in the description is the fruit of focus and analysis that accurately describes not only particular moments of life but what is fundamental in the kind of experience being considered.[5]

The second methodological point requiring elucidation is the turn to experience itself as a source for knowledge and, ultimately, ethical insight. This turn to experience is not unproblematic. To some degree, experience is an unavoidably impure source. Any analysis of experience is itself already conditioned by experience. The very aspects of life that are selected for focus are selected in part on the basis of experience. To make matters worse, we can never step outside experience to determine just how significantly our reflections are conditioned by experience. Conclusions drawn from experience are never completely unsuspect.[6]

This is not to say, however, that there is nothing worthwhile to be gained by turning to experience as a source of knowledge. Indeed, the turn to experience is inescapable. Every other source is also affected by experience,[7] so every caution against the circularity of experience is also needed when turning to other sources, such as scripture, tradition, and reason. Moreover, when we turn to experience to discover more about life, we are turning to a basic source, for we know about life first through our experience of it. Other sources may guide us in our interpretation of experience, but they cannot replace it.

Finally, it must be remembered that the turn to experience is not carte blanche to develop superficial accounts of events or aspects of existence. Insights gained from experience must be subject to tests of their appropriateness. When we develop descriptions of experience, for example, and hold them forth for others to see, we are implying that they have met tests of coherence, accuracy, and precision. That is, they fit and even "make sense" of the fabric of the broader experience of life, especially in light of wisdom from other sources; they are specific and refined, so that others recognize what is being described;[8] and they are repeatable, in that others would themselves repeat the descriptions.[9] What we finally want of a description based on experience is that it resonates with us, that it somehow "rings true." This requires an even stronger match than accuracy, or recognition, because it involves more than our cognitive capacity. When we say that a description rings true to us, we are saying that it touches something in us and that, somehow, it gets something right. This is the final and most important criterion by which we can gauge whether or not a description or account speaks the truth to us.

Finitude

The word 'finitude' calls to mind both the idea that we will die, mortality, and the idea that we are limited. In what follows, an exploration of each is considered to establish the more basic meaning that finitude has for our lives.

Finitude as Mortality

The most profound connection that we make with finitude is the idea of death. When we think of ourselves as finite, we think of ourselves first and foremost as beings who will die, as beings who know that they will die. How do we perceive this mortality? When Shakespeare writes of mortality in his twelfth sonnet, he captures the manner in which this fact of mortality pervades nature and our lives. Writing to his young beauty, he runs through a host of natural images that convince him of his beloved's mortality. He begins with the notion of time and quickly moves to death.

When I do count the clock that tells the time,
And see the brave day sunk in hideous night;
When I behold the violet past prime,
And sable curls all silver'd o'er with white;
When lofty trees I see barren of leaves
Which erst from heat did canopy the herd,
And summer's green all girded up in sheaves
Borne on the bier with white and bristly beard,
Then of thy beauty do I question make,
That thou among the wastes of time must go,
Since sweets and beauties do themselves forsake
And die as fast as they see others grow.[10]

It is the attention that the poet pays to time that provides the initial reminder of death. For us as well as the poet, attention to time reminds us that our days are numbered. The images from nature reinforce this awareness, highlighting its pervasiveness. The setting sun tells us that the time of one day has passed. Faded flowers evoke thoughts of the brevity of a lifespan. And the graying of hair signals that humans, natural beings that we are, also change irrevocably with the passage of time. The beauty of the beloved is thus relativized. It is not eternal. It, too, is subject to the passage of time; it, too, is mortal. Shakespeare closes this sonnet with a couplet that voices a common hope in the face of mortality, immortality: "And nothing 'gainst Time's scythe can make defence / Save breed, to brave him when he takes thee hence."

Shakespeare's sonnet articulates well how the passing of time reminds us of mortality. Ernest Becker makes the same point psychologically when he says that such experiences awaken in us our fear of death.[11] But even if these experiences remind us of death, and even if our most basic fear is of our own mortality, it makes sense not just to look at mortality as the expression of finitude but also to ask what it is about these experiences that connects us with mortality.[12] Is it just that these experiences of the passing of time represent or symbolize mortality for us or is it rather that they, like mortality, are manifestations of the same basic condition? I believe that the latter is the case. Considering the essence of each experience may help us to identify and understand the fundamental condition of existence that they manifest.

Finitude as Limitation

The clock counts the time by marking off the passing of a limited number of hours and minutes of the day. The sun sets each day, signaling the end, the limit, of another day. Flowers fade after they peak; there is a limit to the time of their existence. And even the graying of the hair indicates that there is a limit to the amount of pigmentation for coloring the hair. Every existing thing that the poet refers to and we encounter in the course of our days can be characterized in some respect as limited. What all of these manifest, then, is limitation.

If we move away from the sonnet's images and consider finitude more broadly, we find again that limitation captures the essence of finitude. For example, when Thomas Aquinas argues for the existence of an unlimited being, God, he begins by noticing that *we* have a limited amount of being.[13] No one of us has it all. We do not have to agree with his metaphysics to benefit from his articulation of created being as limited. It is limited in another way, also. We each have our own being, we are each discrete. That is to say, we are limited in such a way that we each have a particular being. I am me and you are you. No matter how emotionally close human beings can become with one another, they are fundamentally separate beings.

In all aspects of our existence, when we bump up against finitude we are experiencing limitation. As Shakespeare reminds us, there is a limit to our days. There is also a limit to the amount of time that we have for doing things. We are limited beings in that just as we cannot be everything so also we cannot do everything. One day's work is only so much work. And along with the limited time that we have to do things, we are limited as to what we can do. We have, that is, finite abilities. We all possess some abilities, but no one person, no matter how talented in how great a variety of areas, possesses all abilities.

There is also a limit to our effectiveness in what we do. For example, the fact that we decide to work very hard at a given task does not mean that we will succeed. Even if we do succeed, our success may well be more modest than what we had hoped for. If our goal is to change the world, we may have to settle for changing only a small part of it. If our aim is to rid the world of a great evil, in all likelihood we will have to be content with reducing the effects of the evil for some. Even a writer as great as Shakespeare cannot move every person to feel what he felt when he created his works.

Limitation and Choices

The very fact that we make choices speaks to the limits of what we can do. We simply cannot affirm and ratify all of the possibilities that we encounter. Many times in the course of our lives, we are presented with the need for choices as to what we will do. At a given point in time, a person can join the military or the Peace Corps, but not both. Even in the minutiae of life, we must choose because of finitude. If we decide to skip lunch in order to reduce our caloric intake, then we cannot at the same time eat lunch. We are limited in such a way that we cannot do all things all at the same time.

We are so limited in this way that we also cannot even affirm all aspects of ourselves at the same time. This is why we each have a finite, developed personality. We must, through the choices that we make—which are in actuality our way of dealing with our basic condition of limitedness—choose who we are and who we will become.[14] Philosophers may debate the genuineness of these choices (are they truly 'free'?), but we can say at a minimum that we experience them as choices that arise from our being limited.

Limitation and Love

Even in the depths of our hearts, in our profoundest moments when we might seem to be finally unlimited beings, we experience limitation. Consider the familiar debate regarding the scope of neighbor love. We may love all people in a general way, and we may be willing to love any person in whatever particular way is appropriate, but we cannot love all persons in this particular and unconditional way.[15] If our particular loves are to be rich, then there must be a limit to their number. Another way of putting this is to say that, although we can love several children specifically, we cannot do the deeds of love[16] for all children of the world.

Likewise in our deep friendships and loves: we must choose/limit our great friends and loves or they will cease to be great. The depth of our love for the truly special people in our lives may seem limitless to us, but the reality is that we can have this kind of love for only a limited number of people in the course of one lifetime. In order to have the experience of limitlessness, then, we must operate within limits. If our loves are to be for us infinitely deep, then they must be finite in number. We are limited beings. We are beings characterized by the necessity of limitation for even our experiences of limitlessness. Our taste of infinity is had in a finite context.

The same can be said of the religious experience of limitlessness. In the classic Christian description of God *via negativa*, we say that God is unlimited. We cannot truly conceptualize infinite and unlimited existence. We have no direct experience of it. What we have, instead, is an intuition or revelation that God is not limited. Our yearning to be with God and share in God's infinity of being is a yearning to transcend the limitation of our own beings, to join with what we have an inkling of, not to participate in something that we can fully conceptualize and understand. We are so deeply limited that we cannot escape the limitation of our thought, even in our thoughts and words about God.

Infinity and Eternity

One final reason exists for identifying limitation as the best explicator of finitude, and that is that limitation captures what underlies the connection between infinity (and immortality) and eternity. A common approach to understanding an idea or concept is to consider its opposite. In the history of the Western world, both infinity and eternity have been paired in opposition to finity. Strictly speaking, infinity is the opposite of finity. It refers to that which is not finite. With respect to existence, it is usually expressed as immortality. Just as finitude closely connects with mortality in our minds, so infinitude closely connects with immortality. It suggests an endlessness, a lack of limitation to the existence of something. The best way to conceptualize this is to think of it in linear terms. What is immortal extends out in time endlessly. One could imagine a timeline of an endless succession of days in the endless life of an immortal being. Similarly, what is infinite extends out linearly without limit, whether it be days or integers. Immortality, after all, refers to an infinite, endless, limitless existence.

Eternal is not the opposite of finite, but it, too, is frequently placed in opposition to what is finite. What distinguishes the eternal from the infinite is that it is free of a different kind of limitation. One could say that the infinite is not limited *with respect to* time. It goes on and on in time. In contrast, what is eternal is not limited *by* time. The eternal is that which exists outside of time.[17] The thing to see regarding finitude is that what makes each an appropriate opposing concept to finitude is a lack of limitation. The infinite is a direct opposite of the finite because both exist in time, while the eternal differs by existing outside of time, but both lack the limitation that is the essence of the concept of finitude.

This description of finitude is itself limited. One can go only so far without considering it in conjunction with contingency, because we experience our finitude as beings who are also contingent. It is necessary, then, to turn now to contingency as a condition of existence and to later return to consider the experience of finitude and contingency as conditions of existence.

Contingency

Like finitude, the word 'contingency' calls to mind more than one way of explicating its meaning as a condition of existence. Contingency as uncertainty and nonnecessity and then contingency as dependency are ideas explored below, once again, as with finitude, to establish the meaning most relevant to our understanding of contingency's fundamental significance for us.

Contingency as Uncertainty and Nonnecessity

The idea of uncertainty most commonly comes to mind when we think of contingency, although the association is not as strong as the one between finitude and mortality. In common parlance, we often use the word *contingency* to describe something about which we are uncertain. We have contingency funds just in case something that might happen actually does. Organizers of complex events make contingency plans if they are cautious. Contracts are made with contingency escape clauses: if the purchaser of a home cannot obtain bank financing by a specified date, the sales contract may be considered null and void. In each of these examples, there is an orientation toward the future. The event is uncertain because it has not yet come to be and it is not certain that it will. Specific future events seem uncertain to us in that it is not inevitable that they come to be.

If we step away from this orientation toward the future and consider the present and even the past, we see that this same uncertainty obtains, but with a different accent. What contingency identifies is not just that something in the future may or may not come to be, but the more basic characteristic that something that was or is or will be did not or does not have to come to be. This is why some philosophers, such as Richard Rorty, tend to prefer understanding contingency as nonnecessity.[18] The aspect of contingency he emphasizes is that the coming to be of a particular event or condition is not (or was not) inevitable because it is part of a grand design or a necessitating metanarrative. It is of note, however, that the logical opposing partner to 'necessary' is 'possible', not 'contingent'.[19] This means that nonnecessity implies possibility, not contingency. The difference here is significant and it explains why both uncertainty and nonnecessity are not entirely satisfactory explicators of contingency. What they both point to is the possibility (rather than the certainty or necessity) of an event occurring, whether in the past, present, or future, but what is missing here is something that is essential to contingency: that something has given rise to the possibility, has shaped the possibility, and plays a role in determining whether or not the possibility will be realized.

Contingency as Dependency

The best way of understanding contingency, a way that captures both the uncertainty and the giving rise to, shaping, and determining possibilities, is as dependency. There is, not surprisingly, good precedent for understanding contingency in this way. The most obvious parallel is in the field of mathematics, where a contingent variable is defined as a dependent variable.[20] In the equation $y = 2x$, y is a contingent variable. Its value depends on the value of x. If x is 2, then y equals 4, but if x is 3, then y equals 6. There is a theological parallel in the Christian doctrine of creation. Here, all of creation is radically dependent on God for the initial act of creation. An even closer parallel is had with the metaphysician's understanding of contingency. When Aquinas writes of the contingency of existence, he is talking about a radical dependence of humanity upon God for each moment of existence. Our existence at each moment is uncertain and it is not necessary (it does not control the free will of God), but even more fundamentally, it is ontologically dependent upon God.[21]

How deep this dependency runs is an open matter. One does not have to agree with Aquinas's metaphysics to recognize that contingency understood as dependency is a fundamental condition of existence. It manifests itself in a variety of ways. The extent of these various forms of dependency in the final analysis may be a matter of judgment, but the presence of dependency itself is evident. At a minimum, there is a sequential dependency. The best way to indicate this is to refer back to the understanding of finitude as limitation. A conceptual line can be drawn from one to the other as follows. Consider physical finitude. We are limited in our existence by time and space. That is, each 'moment' of physical existence can be identified with only one time and one place. This can be described as the singularity of existence as we experience it. Importantly, the singular moments of our experience do not occur in an utterly atomistic and unconnected way. Instead, they occur linearly. Or, more precisely, we do not experience the events as occurring in an utterly atomistic and haphazard way. From the perspective of eternity, that is, from a perspective outside of time, events may just occur. But our experience happens in time and, since the objective here is to describe our experience, language that takes account of the fact that our experience is relative to time is used.

Moreover, this linearity is not just a haphazard collection of independent moments. It is rather a sequentially formed line of events. Our singular experiences, then, can be said to occur sequentially, and it is this sequential aspect of experience that points us to the heart of contingency, because it leads us to see that there is at the very least a sequential dependency of experience. That is to say that a particular experience may not be necessary for the next experience to occur, but it is required for the next experience to have a place in the sequence of a continuous life. To say that what happens to me today is contingent upon what happened to me previously is to say at a minimum that there is this sequential dependency at the heart of the experience of life.[22] Thus, while I might not have purchased a book yesterday *because* I saw a movie the day before, I describe events accurately if I say that I purchased the book the day after I saw the movie, and the possibility of having something happen in its place in the sequence of life depends on other things happening previously.

Understanding finitude as limitation leads conceptually, then, to an understanding of contingency as dependency. It is important to note, however, that the point here is merely a conceptual one. No claim is being made that there is any fundamental or essential priority of finitude to contingency as a condition of existence.

Sequential Dependency

Before considering contingency as dependency in a deeper way, pondering the sequential dependency will help elucidate its significance. What is seen immediately is that the moments of our lives are contextual. Each moment occurs after one and before another. They may seem causally unconnected to us, they may in fact be so, but they do not occur in time unconnectedly. We often speak of an event happening "out of the blue." We mean by that expression that the event was totally unanticipated. We had not been preparing for it, we had not been working to bring it about. We made no choices related to this event. It seems to us to be totally independent of our lives. Yet, how do we identify it as occurring "out of the blue"? We remember what we were doing when it happened and what we did immediately after it happened. We remember it, then, in a context. It struck in the middle of the living of life. We could not experience it if we did not have prior experiences. Its place in our life is dependent upon its place in our lifeline.

With most experiences, this "out of the blue" quality is missing. The more mundane events of our lives occur in a more connected way, in which the sequential dependency merges with a dependency of conditions. For example, the fact that one generally attends high school after grammar school indicates sequence, but also more than a sequential dependency. It indicates that attending grammar school prepares one for high school, that it contributes to the conditions that make attending high school feasible. In most if not all cases, passing grammar school gives rise to the possibility of successfully beginning high school. The dependency here is deeper than mere sequential dependency. It is a dependency of conditions, but it is not of itself a causal dependency, because of course attending grammar school does not cause one to attend high school.

Causal Dependency

In many ways, however, we do experience contingency as a causal dependency. There are times when a specific event in our life causes us to do something that we would not otherwise do. For example, if I break my leg, I will go to the emergency room. My presence in the emergency room will be contingent upon my having broken my leg. I would not be there were it not for the injury. In an example of another type of causal dependency, if I identify activity A (such as studying organic chemistry) as a prerequisite for something B (applying to medical school) that I want to do, then my desire for B causes me to do A. In other words, A has a causal dependency on B (I would not study organic chemistry were it not for my desire to apply to medical school). In this example, we see two types of dependency at work. Not only is A caused by B, but B is conditionally dependent on A. Without A (studying organic chemistry), the conditions do not exist for B (applying to medical school) to occur.

Social Dependency

If we look to the mundane aspects of life, we also find ourselves consistently dependent in a general way on factors we often take for granted. We count on scores of other drivers to obey standard driving rules in order to reach our various destinations safely each day. When we go to the grocery store, we depend on a massive network of farmers and food distributors to put the food we need to purchase on our shelves. This kind of dependency is pervasive, particularly in our complex society of specialization, where each one of us is responsible for a relatively small range of the tasks that go into providing for our sustenance and maintenance.

Personal Dependency

More personally and specifically, we are dependent upon the people in our lives, sometimes in a causal way and sometimes as conditions for the concrete characteristics of our existence. We depend on our parents (causally) for being the particular persons that we are. We need their genes in order to have our particular genetic makeup. Our dependencies upon others for the conditions of the characteristics of our lives are many. If we are to be sisters or brothers, we need siblings to make this the case. If we are to be only children, we cannot have siblings. If we are to be married, we need someone to marry. If we are to parent, we need first someone to complement our role in the procreative process and then we need the child to parent. Should our only child die, for example, then we remain the parent of the deceased child, but we can no longer maintain our identity as a parent of a living child. The day-to-dayness of parenting is no longer possible for us. Similarly, if we are to live in a community, then we need a community in which to live. If we are to be physicians, we need patients so that we can fulfill our role. If we are to be teachers, we depend on the presence of students to teach. We all have a multitude of ways in which we depend on the people in our lives for the very kinds of lives we lead.

These kinds of dependencies make up the fabric of our personal lives. We are enmeshed in life by them. Just as the events of our lives cannot occur for us outside of the sequence of our lives, we cannot be particular social beings without the people who define the kinds of familial and social relationships we have in our lives. We live lives enmeshed in relationships and thus we live lives contingent upon the kinds of relationships we are born into and develop. Our particular identities depend upon those close to us so that we can be who we are in relation to them. In other words, we depend on the people in our lives for the possibilities they give rise to for our lives.

Values and Beliefs

While we sometimes are explicitly aware of these kinds of dependencies in our lives, we experience ourselves as having an inner true self that has a measure of independence from those outside of us, no matter how close they are to us. Whether or not there is a truly independent self is not the question here. What is worth noting, though, is that even our most deeply held values and beliefs, what we identify with our true selves, are at least somewhat dependent on factors outside of ourselves. For example, we may feel that what expresses our innermost being or reality is a belief system that we have taken on, adopted, made our own. Not wanting to discount the self-creation involved in this process, it must be observed that we do not get to create our belief systems *ex nihilo*. At least the foundations of what we believe are part of the givenness of life, whether it be given to us by circumstance of birth or divine revelation. No one whose whole life was lived before Jesus of Nazareth was born, for example, could explicitly and knowingly identify herself or himself as Christian.[23] Even patterns of thought deeply influence what we believe. What we believe, then, is dependent on the context of our lives and on what we experience from without, irrespective of the importance of the creative contributions we make to this givenness.[24]

Contingency as dependency, like finitude as limitation, profoundly characterizes our existence. Every aspect of our lives is affected by this contingency. Yet, were we only contingent and not also finite, this contingency might not matter so much. If our lives were of unlimited duration and possibility, then the pervasiveness of our dependency would matter little, at least theoretically, because given enough time and opportunity we would experience such a range of contexts that at some point we would transcend each particular dependency. The rub is that we are both limited and dependent.

We never actually experience one condition without the other. So to do justice to the experience of life, it is necessary to attempt a description of the experience of finitude and contingency, despite the conceptual difficulties.

The Experience of Finitude and Contingency

It is our being finite that makes our contingency matter so much to us. Consider genetic dependency. Why does it matter so much to me what genes my parents gave me? It matters because my genetic makeup is limited. I get only one. I do not get this genetic makeup now and at the same time another one. I do not get to be me and you. I only get to be me, so my dependency upon my parents for causing me to have my particular complex of genes is tremendously important. The same can be seen in a consideration of finitude. Why does my being limited in any particular respect matter so much to me? It matters because this limitation will play a role in giving rise to, shaping, and determining the possibilities that will be realized in me and my life. If I cannot sing, a career on the Broadway stage is out for me. If I cannot abide laboratory work, then all of the career paths in the research sciences are closed to me. Less negatively, if I cannot speak well extemporaneously, wanting to circumvent this limitation may encourage me to develop skills at preparing speeches, which may lead to a career as a speechwriter for others. I am, in other words, dependent upon the limitations of my existence to the same extent that I am limited in my dependencies.

Mind and Consciousness

In the process of living, however, we do not experience the limited dependencies and dependent limitations so much as we experience ourselves as both limited and dependent at the same time. We may at times be more aware of some limitations or dependencies than others as the events of our lives call our attention to them, but we live our lives as limited and dependent beings. Even our observations reflect this. Consider for a moment the conceptual move to consider finitude and contingency separately. In order to understand our reflections on experience, we are dependent upon the capacities of our mind. But these capacities on which we depend are themselves limited, and so we must find ways to limit what we attempt to conceive. To start out with finitude and contingency together would be mentally overwhelming without first describing carefully what each is. The capacity for understanding on which we depend requires a limitation of scope to be efficacious. Similarly, the conceptual tools that we bring to bear are both dependent and limited-dependent on the tools we are aware of and trained in and limited in the kinds of tools that are effective for us in helping us to understand. The fact that limitation and dependency characterize our existence means that they are conditions that must be reckoned with in every aspect of our lives, even reflection on our lives.

If we take this one step further, we see that even conscious experience itself is both finite and contingent. It is limited in that each one of us has only so much of it. I can only be conscious, first of all, of *my* experience and, second, of a limited amount of experience at a time. It is contingent in that what comes into consciousness for each of us is dependent sequentially, conditionally, causally, and contextually in myriad ways—on our minds, experiences, friends and relatives, opportunities, and limitations. Moreover, the very fact that I have conscious experiences on which I reflect (including the process of reflection itself) manifests both limitation and dependency. To the extent to which it is developed to a uniquely human degree, it is limiting: it sets me apart from other animals as a defining characteristic of human beingness. My being human is at least dependent upon my capacity for this human consciousness, as are a whole range of human experiences that require reflective consciousness for them to be what they are to me.[25] Thus, human consciousness both functions in a limited and dependent way and is itself a limiting and dependent characteristic of human existence.

If something so basic as human consciousness itself exhibits finitude and contingency, then every aspect of existence I experience as a conscious being is filtered by these characteristics because I am aware of my experiences only through my consciousness.[26] This alone makes the limitation and dependency of human consciousness significant. What makes it even more important is that it is through human consciousness that I am aware of the conditions of my existence. As Ernest Becker notes, it is unique to humans to live life knowing that they will die,[27] and this knowledge is had through human consciousness. Similarly, although we are not always consciously aware of finitude and contingency as conditions of existence, what awareness we do have of them is had through our consciousness. Our awareness, then, is characterized by finitude and contingency itself: we cannot be fully aware, and what awareness we do have is dependent upon our abilities, past experiences, and so on. Our conscious experience of and reflection upon finitude and contingency is thus itself limited and contingent.

Possibilities

At every turn, we experience the limitations and dependencies of existence as intertwined. We are dependent upon our very limitations. We are limited by our dependencies. The effect is in some ways constraining. My limitations may determine my possibilities, and so I am dependent upon them for what I can and cannot do. My dependencies, on my parents for my genetic makeup, for one example, give rise to the very limitations on which I subsequently depend. Both my dependencies and my limitations mark off which possibilities arise and which do not arise for me in my life. However, the effect of being thus limited and dependent is also in some ways liberating. After all, this marking off is of the *possibilities* for me in my life. Without the limitations, without the specific dependencies, no possibilities could arise.[28]

The individual descriptions of finitude and contingency come together at this point. In experience, both limitation and dependency are at work in the specific life I live. For example, finitude makes choice necessary. I cannot do all things at once and so I must choose. What arise as real possibilities for me to choose among, however, are contingent. In other words, that I must choose reflects the finite nature of existence; that I have specific options to choose among reflects the contingent nature of existence.

If we look at our loves, we see this interplay at work. As noted in the section on finitude, if we are to love deeply, we must limit our loves. We simply do not have an endless amount of time on this earth to love every person concretely and in depth. Which persons we do love and the kinds of people whom we can be in relation to in our loves, however, is determined by the contingent nature of life. Our own particularities, our own desires and personalities, play a role in determining who we will love in a deep way. More than that, the particularities of others' lives will also play a role in determining who will be present for us to love. Our loves are limited and dependent, yet they are made possible by the particular limitations and dependencies of our own and of those we encounter in life.

We can see the same intertwining in our spiritual lives. It may well be that it is our awareness of our finitude that turns us to the infinite, making us long for transcendence of this aspect of life. But how we turn, how we interpret the infinite, even how we worship the divine is profoundly dependent upon the givenness of our particular life, time of life, and place of life.

Vulnerability

What this means for the experience of life is a profound vulnerability to the conditions of existence. Everything that I experience is either itself finite and contingent[29] or experienced finitely and contingently through consciousness.[30] Everything that I am, that I experience myself to be, is also, at least to some degree, finite and contingent. I would not be a specific me were it not for finitude. I would not be specifically myself were it not for contingency. At each step in life, what I experience is affected by these conditions of existence. Most deeply, I am dependent upon a finite number of people for the richness of my life. I am dependent upon others for the support of my existence, for food, shelter, work, leisure activity, and society. Moreover, if in conjunction with this I note that I am particular but not unique, then I logically see others not only as beings on whom I depend, but also as people who depend upon me. For as I reflect on the limited and dependent nature of my existence, I recognize that others also experience these conditions and I must acknowledge that others are dependent in particular ways upon me.

In the nexus of existence, then, we experience ourselves as limited by and dependent upon other persons and events outside of ourselves and we experience ourselves as beings who at times limit others, because we are beings on whom others depend. For example, my children have their genetic makeup in part because of the particular genes I gave to them. Beyond this, they will live where I live and they will be shaped by my values, my personality, and my choices. I am not the only limiting factor in their lives on which they depend, but I am an important one. This creates in me a sense of responsibility toward them, to live where I want them to live, to have values I want them to see, to make choices with their welfare in mind. In other words, this means that I am also vulnerable to their dependence upon me. What is more, they are not the only people to whom I have responsibilities. How I am able to meet my specific responsibilities toward my children must depend on the entire fabric of my life and my total mix of obligations toward others and myself.

The conditions of existence impinge upon us in a highly complex way. The sorrows of life bear their mark, be it hunger, imprisonment, death, lost love, being overburdened or overworked, being poor, or being oppressed. It might be tempting at this point to recede into resignation. We are all so vulnerable to finitude and contingency, understood as limitation and dependency, that we feel helpless. And yet, these very same conditions of existence are what make us *not* helpless, for they are what define and shape both our capacities and the nature of life such that others are vulnerable to *us*. Feelings of helplessness must wrestle with feelings of power. We know that we can affect others, we know that decisions we make about how we are to live are not made in isolation, touching us alone.

Our inclination to think of our vulnerability solely as a weakness comes from our tendency to understand it as a capacity for being harmed. If, however, we understand it more openly as our capacity to be affected by what happens to us, then we see that vulnerability is a neutral term. We can think of a piece of sculpture, a beautiful work of art. Yes, the sculpture is vulnerable to a hammer if it is struck with force. In this case, the vulnerability allows destruction. But the sculpture was also vulnerable to the sculptor's hand and eye; it would never have had its beauty were it not for this constructive vulnerability. The same is true of us. Just as we are vulnerable to the conditions of our existence such that they limit and constrain us, we are vulnerable to them such that they also define and shape us and the possibilities of our lives. Generally, our response to being vulnerable to finitude and contingency is to try to protect ourselves from them, and this response is often appropriate. Daily functioning is facilitated by not always facing our vulnerability. Our strategies for protecting ourselves generally revolve around our conceptions of genuine human freedom vis-à-vis the conditions of existence, falling into two classes: denial and resignation. When we overstate the degree of genuine human freedom vis-à-vis the conditions of existence, we engage in denial. The existentialist who envisions persons as always standing with the possibility of complete self-negation/self-creation is an example of this form. We also secure a degree of protection when we understate our freedom. Fate protects us. Everything that is must be, and we resign ourselves to it. Yet, despite the apparent benefits of such protective measures, it is also the case that we need to be open to our vulnerability, and that of others, to the conditions of our existence, for it is a potentially constructive as well as destructive vulnerability. And so, to experience and understand life as it is, to gain the moral knowledge we seek, we need also to resist both denial and resignation.

This understanding of the human person as finite and contingent, as a being who experiences life as finitely contingent and contingently finite, opens the way for us to begin to come to grips with our vulnerability to the conditions of existence, as well as the possibilities for action it creates for us. As soon as we see this, however, we must grapple with the underlying assumption that we have the capacity to choose how to act in relation to the possibilities created for us. For this, an examination of the way we have thought and, more importantly, could think about human freedom is in order.

Notes

1. Vulnerability generally refers to our capacity for being harmed, in both physical and nonphysical ways (see *Oxford English Dictionary*, 2d ed., New York: Oxford University Press, 1989, s.v. "vulnerability" and "vulnerable"). However, what I am getting at with the term 'vulnerability' is that we can be affected, shaped, and changed by what happens to us or by what we come up against, even when it is the result of our own choice.

2. Paul Ricoeur, *Fallible Man*, trans. Charles Kelbley (Chicago: Henry Regnery, 1965), 3.

3. For a poignant description of the psychological struggle engendered by our finitude, see Ernest Becker, *The Denial of Death* (New York: Free Press, 1973), 25–30.

4. To understand the difference between the present, constructive approach and more typical approaches, consider two examples. In ancient times, Stoic philosophers attempted to incorporate finitude and contingency (fate) into their understandings of human nature and morality, but they were not asking the same kinds of questions, especially regarding obligation, as I am. See J. M. Rist, *Stoic Philosophers* (New York: Cambridge University Press, 1969), 112–22. In recent times, Paul Tillich has also dealt substantially with finitude and contingency, but with theological, not ethical, concerns. See Tillich, *The Courage to Be* (New Haven, Conn.: Yale University Press, 1952), 42–45. In a contemporary work, Alasdair MacIntyre does treat dependence as "central to the human condition," but he does so in relation to human rationality. See MacIntyre, *Dependent Rational Animals* (Chicago: Open Court, 1999), 4–5.

5. This account of the descriptive task bears similarity to that given by Herbert Spiegelberg in *The Phenomenological Movement* (Boston: Martinus Nijhoff, 1982), 682, but it is not restricted, as his is, to phenomenological descriptions.

6. Paul Lauritzen approaches the difficulties of appealing to experience as well as the importance of doing so from a different but instructive angle in "Hear No Evil, See No Evil, Think No Evil: Ethics and the Appeal to Experience," *Hypatia* 12, no. 2 (Spring 1997): 93–103.

7. For an account of the complex interaction of experience with other sources for ethics, see, for example, Margaret Farley's "The Role of Experience in Moral Discernment," in *Christian Ethics: Problems and Prospects*, ed. Lisa Sowle Cahill and James F. Childress (Cleveland: Pilgrim, 1996), 135–36.

8. Margaret Farley also includes coherence and recognition among her more comprehensive list of guiding criteria, though she identifies them somewhat differently. See Farley, "Role of Experience," 146.

9. Accuracy and precision are common metrological standards. Accuracy refers to a measurement matching the measuring standard, while precision refers to the degree of repeatability of that match. A measuring machine is said to be accurate if its measurement of a standard closely matches the value of the standard; it is said to be precise if it is able to replicate that measurement repeatedly. Obviously, descriptions of experience are not appropriate objects for measuring machines, but when we seek to evaluate a description, we are trying to assess its "measure."

10. William Shakespeare, sonnet XII, *The Complete Works of Shakespeare*, ed. Hardin Craig and David Bevington (Glenview, Ill.: Scott, Foresman, 1951), 473.

11. Becker asserts that "it is life itself" that awakens our fear of death. *Denial of Death*, 66.

12. Paul Ricouer's observation that no one alive has an experience of her own death reminds us that we can only connect these experiences with the idea of death. Ricoeur, *Freedom and Nature: The Voluntary and the Involuntary*, trans. Erazim V. Kohák (Evanston, Ill.: Northwestern University Press, 1966), 456–67.

13. Thomas Aquinas, *Summa Theologica*, trans. Fathers of the English Dominican Province (Westminster, Md.: Christian Classics, 1948), I, 7, 1–3.

14. See Ernest Becker, *The Revolution in Psychiatry* (New York: Free Press, 1964), 65, for a psychological development of this point. For a philosophical version, see Harry Frankfort's *The Importance of What We Care About: Philosophical Essays* (New York: Cambridge University Press, 1988).

15. Gene Outka makes this point regarding the scope of neighbor love in *Agape: An Ethical Analysis* (New Haven, Conn.: Yale University Press, 1972), 269.

16. The terminology is Margaret Farley's.

17. I am indebted here to Hannah Arendt's insightful analysis of the distinction between immortality and eternality in Greek thought, in *The Human Condition* (Chicago: University of Chicago Press, 1958), 18–21.

18. Richard Rorty, *Philosophy and the Mirror of Nature* (Princeton, N.J.: Princeton University Press, 1979), 169. Also see D. W. Hamlyn, "Contingent and Necessary Statements," in *The Encyclopedia of Philosophy*, ed. Paul Edwards (New York: Macmillan; Free Press, 1967), and *The Dictionary of Religion and Philosophy*, ed. Geddes MacGregor (New York: Paragon House, 1989), s.v. "Contingency."

19. See A. N. Prior, "Logic Model," in *Encyclopedia of Philosophy*. For an example of the possible used in opposition to the necessary, see Aquinas, *Summa Theologica*, I, 2, 3. The Stoic philosophers Cleanthes and Chrysippus also thought of nonnecessity as possibility, according to J. M. Rist, in *Stoic Philosophy*, 117 and 121. Also, Søren Kierkegaard pairs the necessary and the possible in his discussion of God's will in *Sickness Unto Death*, trans. Walter Lowrie (Princeton, N.J.: Princeton University Press, 1954), 174.

20. Similarly, in the field of statistics a contingency table classifies the degree of dependence of attributes. See Murray Spiegel, *Schaum's Outline of Theory and Problems of Statistics* (New York: McGraw-Hill, 1961), 204.

21. Aquinas says in *Summa Theologica*, I, 8, 1, "[A]s long as a thing has being, God must be present to it, according to its mode of being." Also see Paul Davies, *The Mind of God* (New York: Simon & Schuster, 1992), 69, for his description of ontological contingency.

A more general version of this metaphysical understanding of dependency can be found in the more primitive stories of dependency for existence on the spirit world, as well as in contemporary theories in physics, in particular atomic physics, that find in the breakdown of atoms into energy the grounds for supposing that "our physical form emanates from an unknown dimension which sustains it." See Ernest Becker, *The Birth and Death of Meaning* (New York: Free Press, 1971), 119–21.

While there is no one version of this story of dependency that satisfies all, there does appear to be a general consensus that, since we cannot account for our coming into being and continuing in being ourselves, we are ontologically dependent beings.

22. Interestingly, Ernest Becker argues that recognizing the linearity of experience is what led to the development of contemporary human consciousness and so is at the very center of what it means to be a human person. See *Revolution*, 23, 27–29.

23. We can prescind here from considering Karl Rahner's notion of the Anonymous Christian, presented in "Anonymous Christian," *Theological Investigations*, vol. 6, trans. Karl-H. Kruger and Boniface Kruger (New York: Seabury, 1974), 390–98.

24. It is difficult to discuss this point without resorting to notions of an inner self and separations of the self and what is given. Postmodern philosophers have challenged this way of viewing the 'self' so persuasively that it is not possible to ignore this challenge as one of the givens to a person writing at this point in time. Still, for the purposes here, it is useful to hold onto some common expression of the inner self interacting with context, even though this way of referring to it may be open to challenge. In chapters 2 and 3, I make my case that the self is not merely a fiction used to describe an utterly contingent and constructed being.

25. This is true even if my particular capacity is impaired, as through a coma, or damaged, as by brain injury, because I am the kind of being who has this capacity. Whether or not impairment or damage can ever be so extensive as to render me outside the species or category of human being is a complex question requiring more exploration than is possible here.

26. Unconscious experience is clearly beyond the scope of this work, so it is not considered. Earlier, in the sections on finitude and contingency, features of existence not dependent on consciousness were considered. They are still in play. The point here is that the focus on experience is a focus on conscious experience.

27. Becker, *Denial of Death*, 26–27.

28. See William Lynch, *Images of Hope* (Baltimore: Helicon Press, 1965), especially pages 72–80, for an insightful rendering of how limitation creates possibility, or the awareness of possibility, and the importance of this for psychological well-being.

29. A common assertion in Christian theology is that God is the one case in which these predicates likely do not obtain.

30. Even God is experienced finitely and contingently through consciousness.

CHAPTER TWO

Freedom and Personhood in a Non-Newtonian Paradigm

If we think of finitude and contingency as fundamental conditions of existence that give rise to and shape the possibilities for our lives, then we are already assuming that they do not fully determine our lives. We are assuming, in other words, that human persons are not only finite and contingent, but also free. Moreover, ethics as a discipline has traditionally assumed some role for choice in the moral life.[1] Questions regarding responsibility for actions, the necessity for deliberation in making choices, character development, and moral assessment of human actions, for example, all assume the existence of some capacity for freedom. At the current time, however, it is not adequate to adopt a model of human existence that simply identifies human freedom as a substantive or real capacity. To speak of human persons as free in a meaningful way, then, requires justification. Yet dismissing the possibility of human freedom is also problematic, because it not only undermines our ability to engage in ethical analysis, but it also defies what is generally considered a part of human experience. Whether or not we actually are free, in a real sense, we experience ourselves as having the ability to make choices between options, choices that may be profoundly shaped by factors in our existence but that are not wholly determined by them.

This state of affairs leaves the ethicist in a quandary of sorts. Ultimately, genuine human freedom cannot be proven or disproved, so no easy resolution exists to this quandary. However, it might be possible to move forward and say something about human freedom if we examine both a view of the human person as free and a view that does not include human freedom in order to recognize what the strengths, weaknesses, and underlying assumptions are for each view. The goal of this endeavor is to identify a new paradigm for thinking about human freedom that allows us to articulate a view of the human person that fits with our understanding of the conditions of existence. To do this, we must identify first what is problematic in the entire approach taken to the question of human freedom since the eighteenth century. This can be achieved by comparing the positions of two major thinkers who are representative of lines of thought that challenge one another in key ways on what it is to be a human person, yet share the same problematic in their approach to the question on the whole. Roman Catholic theologian Karl Rahner and modern pragmatist philosopher Richard Rorty have dealt substantively with the questions at hand from virtually opposite ends of the spectrum. Interestingly, they have done so with complementary foci. Rahner deals directly with the issue of human freedom in his theological anthropology, while Rorty sets aside the question of personal freedom and examines human contingency. For Rahner, the understanding of the human person as free is foregrounded and reflections on human contingency are less direct. Rorty, for his part, calls attention to human contingency, viewing it as so total that the human person is said to be socially constructed through and through, but he offers no explicit philosophical anthropology. To bring the thought of the two into conversation, the complementary aspects of each figure's view must be made explicit, so that the key assumptions of each can be examined and challenged for what they have to offer for understanding the operative overarching paradigm of human action and what that suggests about the need for a new paradigm.

Before turning to the specific anthropologies in Rahner's and Rorty's thought, however, it might be beneficial to say something about the problem of dealing with freedom that has beset Western thought since the eighteenth century, a problem that both of these thinkers share, albeit in different ways. Succinctly, that problem has been Newtonian mechanistic determinism. From the dawn of modernity, philosophical and religious thought has had to come to grips with science as the new authority. Since the time of Pascal and the new probability theory, credibility goes not to what is 'probable', as in provable by appeal to an established authority, such as the Roman Catholic church or a philosophical 'truth', but to what is most likely to be 'true' according to the canons of modern science.[2] The positions regarding the relationship of religious claims to science vary, but for religious claims to be engaged seriously, they too must carefully delineate their relationship to scientific knowledge. The most persuasive types of claims, of course, are those that do not contradict science.[3] From Newton onward, philosophers and theologians alike have asked their questions about freedom with the presumption that their answers must somehow accommodate or not contradict mechanistic determinism. In the case of Rahner, an accommodation is made; in the case of Rorty, a concession of freedom is made so that no contradiction can arise. Indeed, Rorty embraces this concession and a form of mechanism, despite his suggesting in *Objectivity, Relativism, and Truth* that the opposition of freedom to mechanism is misplaced.[4] But there may be another approach that is available. While more will be said in the fourth section of this chapter, it is important to note now that the world of science experienced a genuine paradigm shift early in the twentieth century, the ramifications of which are just being felt now at all levels of existence. The most important ramification for the matter at hand is that mechanistic determinism is not the near absolute roadblock to freedom that it was once thought to be. And if that is the case, then it may also be defensible to speak of genuine human freedom without contradicting the major scientific worldview of our time.

In the first two sections that follow, I offer accounts of Rahner's and Rorty's anthropologies and their understandings of human dependency, or contingency, vis-à-vis freedom. Then in the third section I bring the two thinkers into conversation, both to see what they can add to an understanding of the human person and to identify the ways in which mechanistic determinism affects the thought of these radically different thinkers. In the final section, I offer a new way of considering human freedom that does not contradict what science since Einstein adds to the conversation.

Rahner's Anthropology

Although Karl Rahner consistently refers to his understanding of the human person throughout his massive corpus, nowhere does he do so with more concentration on specifically developing an anthropology than in *Foundations of Christian Faith*. The account presented here, then, is taken mainly from this work. It should be noted that *Foundations* is an introduction to theology and, for Rahner, anthropology is the starting point. As he observes early in his introduction to *Foundations*, "Every theology, of course, is always a theology which arises out of the secular anthropologies and self-interpretations of man."[5] While all theologies begin with the question about what it is to be a human being, what is distinct for Rahner about Christian theology is that it is "the answer to the question that man is," "the universal question which he is for himself."[6] And it is in the juxtaposition of this question and answer that the "transcendental and historical conditions which make revelation possible"[7] are found. But as we examine Rahner's thought here, we will see the difficulties that emerge with his way of viewing the human person and features of being human, such as freedom. First, however, key aspects of his anthropology need to be considered.

Transcendental Experience

What does Rahner mean when he says that the human person is a question for herself? Simply put, he means that this is how the human person experiences her whole self. As Anne Carr points out, this is the "experience of subjectivity."[8] It is the experience of herself as subject. This experience of self as subject is central to Rahner's anthropology. For Rahner, viewing the human creature as person and subject, with an historically constituted essential being, is crucial for both "the possibility of Christianity and the self-understanding of Christianity."[9] All of the core Christian assertions, such as the possibility of a personal relationship with God, individual salvation, and responsibility before God, depend for Rahner on such a self-understanding.

To explain what he means by the experience of self as person and subject, Rahner first considers that the human being experiences herself "as the product of that which is not [her]self."[10] The empirical sciences, for example, represent legitimate but insufficient attempts by human beings to explain themselves by these outside causes. Rahner elaborates on the significance of this phenomenon. He points out that it is precisely in this experience of being caused by outside factors that the human being experiences herself as person and subject, because the very fact that she knows this, has this experience, is not itself explained by these causes.[11] Moreover, in raising analytical questions about herself, in opening herself to the "unlimited horizons of such questions," the human being transcends herself.[12] In this experience, what Rahner calls the "transcendental experience,"[13] the human person affirms herself as more than the individual, analyzable components of her reality.[14] It is important to note, however, that Rahner does not devalue these determining components of reality. What he asserts is that the human being experiences herself as more than the sum of these components. This is why he says that the empirical sciences endeavor *legitimately* to explain humanity by studying these components. Rahner's point is that they will never explain *all* of the human being, never fully explain the human being's ability to experience herself as subject.

In this experience of being a questioning self, in experiencing herself as a question *for* herself, the human person also experiences her horizon as infinite.[15] For every question the human person asks of herself is asked within a horizon. And every answer, even a finite answer, within one horizon becomes another question within a larger horizon. In this ever-expanding way, the human person experiences herself as existing within an infinite horizon. Similarly, within this infinite horizon, the human person also experiences herself as having "infinite possibility," because every answer to every question simultaneously becomes a new question and a new possibility. And with this infinite possibility, the person experiences herself as spirit.

Crucially, however, the person has this experience in and through her finite reality. In the experience of transcendence, then, the human person experiences herself as both spirit and finite reality. Transcendence is thus not separable from finite reality. It is instead a "mode of being" that is "prior to and permeates every objective experience."[16] Transcendence itself is always present in the "background" of life.[17]

Freedom

The transcendental experience also reveals to the human person that she is responsible and free. Because the human person experiences herself as subject, the transcendental realities of responsibility and freedom are also experienced.[18] The human person knows herself to be responsible because she experiences herself as "consigned" to herself, responsible not only for her knowledge but also for her actions.[19] And when this self-responsibility is ultimate, when it is both for one's knowledge as self-consciousness and for one's actions as self-actualization, it is what Rahner calls "transcendental freedom."[20]

Transcendental freedom, as a transcendental reality, is not experienced directly; rather, it is "always mediated by the concrete realities of time and space, of man's material and history."[21] To distinguish transcendental freedom from mediated freedom, Rahner calls the former "originating" and the latter "originated." He emphasizes, however, that the two are "two moments which form the single unity of freedom." Thus, although freedom is grounded in the person's transcendental essence, it is experienced by concrete individuals each with a particular location in the world, in time, and in history. These aspects of particular location are also aspects of a person's subjectivity, and it is only through these aspects that the person is able to realize her transcendental freedom. Thus a person's transcendental essence and her existential reality are intrinsically and reciprocally linked.[22]

Contingency

For Rahner, human freedom exists ultimately for human salvation, for it is only through a free act of acceptance of self and God that one is able to gain a final and eternal validity for one's existence.[23] Yet the human person does not experience herself as only free. She also experiences herself as dependent even in her freedom. Attempts to explain herself by external causes, for example, reflect this experience of dependency. And the way in which she experiences herself as more than the sum of the effects of external causes tells her that she is a self, responsible and free. However, Rahner argues that the human person does not experience this self as the *cause* of her transcendental self, and this awareness that she is not the cause brings her the recognition that she is "in the presence of being as mystery." This is how she knows herself to be "established by and at the disposal of another, . . . grounded in ineffable mystery."[24] This ineffable mystery, which establishes and grounds each human person, is God. Because the human person feels herself thus radically dependent on God, she experiences herself as oriented toward God.[25]

While Rahner does not expressly consider contingency as a feature of human existence, he does take account of it in two ways. First, he points to the heart of the contingency of existence with his conception of the human person as fundamentally dependent on God as the ground and horizon of being. He thus captures radical dependency (contingency) at the level of existence. Second, he takes account of contingency in his emphasis on human beings as historically constituted beings. Clearly, Rahner presents a view of human persons as deeply but not wholly vulnerable to the conditions of their existence. Recall that for Rahner one is spirit and finite at one and the same time, not a spirit with a body or a body with a spirit. As each person acts in time to exercise her ultimate freedom for self-disposition toward or away from mystery, the individual, particular aspects of her existence share in the eternal validity of her self-disposition. Who she definitively is, how she stands before the mystery that we call God, is not separable from her concrete existence. Her identity, including her eternal self, is thus deeply vulnerable to the concrete aspects of her life.

Rahner connects freedom with contingency, then, by viewing the human person as free in and through the concrete aspects of her existence, aspects on which she depends for her particular identity. He also sees the human person as vulnerable to that freedom, both one's own and that of others. Who we are as human beings, therefore, depends not solely on knowable and predictable contingent factors, but also on that which is in principle unknowable: God and the results of free actions.

Rorty's Anthropology

It must be acknowledged from the start that it is not Richard Rorty's specific aim to develop an anthropology that is based on pragmatist philosophy. Indeed, it is more accurate to say that it is his specific aim *not* to develop an anthropology. As Charles Taylor notes, one of the questions Rorty seeks to put aside is, What is the nature of self-understanding?[26] And Rorty himself classifies "the nature of man" as an "unprofitable topic."[27] This position follows directly from the pragmatist commitment to changing the questions that philosophy asks. From *Philosophy and the Mirror of Nature* through *Objectivity, Relativism, and Truth* and *Contingency, Irony, and Solidarity*, Rorty mounts a consistent effort to rid Western philosophy of its entanglement in questions that, to his mind, have preoccupied us to no advantage. For example, he sees all attempts to find a realist ground for arguing for human rights as misguided, because they require "a God's-eye point of view," a "skyhook" that could free us from our particularized points of view.[28]

What Rorty wishes to substitute for realist grounds is social agreement. He calls this "epistemological behaviorism," in which social agreement rather than philosophical theory or any other belief structure is authoritative.[29] Rorty insists that instead of attempting to discover philosophical truths to ground our beliefs, we should accept that the philosophical task is one of creation/edification.[30] He argues that we make beliefs true by deciding "what it is better for us to believe," not by deciding how to behave based on what we discover to be true.[31] Rorty has thus given up on discovering 'Truth'. His goal is to convince us that social harmony will be better advanced by increasing our capacity to tolerate diversity through shared and expanded experiences of culture than by seeking to "use universalistic notions like 'the nature of the self' or 'our essential humanity' as fulcrums for criticism of current moral convictions or social institutions."[32] His approach is behavioral and historicist, not metaphysical. Thus, any construal of what it means to be a human person that goes beyond description of a particular person or culture is ruled out of order.

Decisional Personhood

However true to pragmatist values it may be for Rorty to put aside questions about the nature of the human person, the fact remains that underlying his own philosophical project is a particular view of the human person. While Rorty insists that what he has to say does not apply to "the" human person, he does betray a generalized view of human persons. Lifting up the embedded elements of his philosophical anthropology, then, is a task that must be undertaken with caution. The fact that Rorty opposes the very idea of a pragmatist anthropology means that, in order to articulate one, the account that follows must at times be adversarial to Rorty's stated position. In other words, unlike Rahner, Rorty's claim that there is no 'self' on which to base an anthropology has to be challenged in order to argue that underlying his position is indeed a view of the human person that is philosophically significant as an anthropology. Rorty's flair for the rhetorical can also complicate this endeavor. We need to see exactly what it is that Rorty says or implies about human persons without being misled by his command of words. For example, the fact that he judges explorations of what it means to be a human person unprofitable does not entail the claim that the exploration is meaningless: just that the meaning, if there is one, is elusive. We have to look precisely at what Rorty says about human persons and what his conception of contingency implies about human freedom to get a fair representation of his philosophical anthropology.

What we find is a view of the human person that involves at its heart a decision as to who counts as a person. In *Contingency, Irony, and Solidarity*, Rorty argues that we must acknowledge that we do not have a "common human nature."[33] This is because, as he argues in *Philosophy and the Mirror of Nature*, "personhood" is "a matter of decision rather than knowledge, an acceptance of another human being into fellowship rather than a recognition of a common essence."[34] The only quality that Rorty allows as a shared element is our common susceptibility to humiliation, the one form of pain that we do not share with other animals.[35] Yet possession of this common element is not sufficient to make someone a person. The decision must still be made to recognize a specific being as possessing that quality. His goal is to increase the numbers of beings we include in this group called human persons, and he thinks that we can accomplish this only by means of imaginative identification,[36] whereby we come to view our differences with others as less significant than our "similarities with respect to pain and humiliation."[37] This does not involve any appeals to human dignity, capacity for transcendence, value by God, recognition of dependency, or awe in the face of mystery. It involves instead an assessment that the details of another's life may be similar enough to one's own, especially with respect to humiliation, that we decide to see this other as more like ourselves, and thus a person, than as different.

What is key for Rorty here is that we have no such thing as a common human nature that would compel others, sooner or later, to recognize our humanity and to treat us accordingly. This is not because Rorty does not care about how we treat one another. It is rather because he worries that what we find when we look for markers of humanity is nothing else but what we have put there, and thus our construals of common human nature are ineluctably culture bound. They are also just as likely as any pragmatist construal to be exclusionary and arbitrary.[38] This is why Rorty insists that there is "nothing deep down inside us except what we have put there ourselves."[39] Personhood refers not to intrinsic features or capacities, to anything 'real' that we need to look harder at to see more clearly, but to inclusion in the group of beings counted as full human persons. This makes personhood decisional and possibly even communitarian, but not inherent.

As we become persuaded that there is no such thing as a common human nature, we also come to recognize that we do not have anything like a 'self'. For if there is nothing inside us except what we have put there ourselves, then what we call a self is an illusion, a trope for our social construction. Indeed, in Rorty's view we are "socially constructed all the way down."[40] This is the final 'truth' about ourselves. What Rorty does not satisfactorily explain is how this 'truth' claim differs from the truth claims made by realists open to metaphysical interpretations of human nature. One of the troubling rhetorical aspects to Rorty's writing is his continual use of the pronoun "we." While Rorty finds no common human nature, he does "discover" the truth about "us," and this may not be metaphysical but it is hard to see how it is not realist or representationalist at its most fundamental level.

At times, Rorty hedges on his claims regarding human persons. For example, consider his claim that we are socialized all the way down along with a second claim. The first indicates his view that there is nothing to being a human person except what society tells us we are, from the outside, which we then internalize. But the second claim seems designed to undercut this. In his introduction to *Contingency, Irony, and Solidarity*, where he is perhaps taking a conciliatory tack in trying to make the pragmatist project convincing, he asserts,

> To say that there is no such thing as intrinsic nature is not to say that the intrinsic nature of reality has turned out, surprisingly enough, to be extrinsic. It is to say that the term "intrinsic nature" is one which it would pay us not to use, an expression which has caused us more trouble than it is worth. . . . But this claim about the relative profitability, in turn, is just the recommendation that we in fact *say* little about these topics, and see how we get on.[41]

These two claims simply do not mesh. One must look to the balance of his work to decide the matter. Is Rorty merely changing the subject, as his second claim suggests, or is he saying that the subject in fact is different than Western philosophy has taken it to be? The balance of his work clearly supports the view that Rorty is not referring to the profitability of philosophical discourse when he boldly claims that "there is nothing deep down inside us except what we have put there ourselves." He is saying rather that the intrinsic nature of reality has turned out to be extrinsic.

Given Rorty's rhetorical style, which is intended to persuade, it is difficult at times to resist the temptation to counter his persuasive tone. However, something important is missed if the reader gives in to this temptation without further consideration. Rorty does not insist on the importance of social construction of the self merely to be argumentative or to present an elegant phrase. He does it to do justice to the experience of being caused, and he attempts this in a framework that sees causes and effects as indistinguishable links in a single chain. More will be said regarding the significance of this for predictability, but for now it is important to note that Rorty's insistence that we stop thinking of the self as having a status independent of external causes is a serious effort to stop viewing the self as capable of stepping outside of contingent human existence.

Freedom

There are, however, two consequences to viewing the human person as a being who has simply internalized the external. The first is that there is no longer any meaningful way to construe the 'self' as an enduring identity that goes beyond the continuity of a physical being's history. Indeed, Rorty presents this as a virtue of the position. The second is that the human person is totally vulnerable to contingency and finitude. Interestingly enough, both consequences point to the same vital feature in Rorty's philosophical anthropology: there is no place for genuine, creative human freedom in his understanding of the human person. In this section, we will look at the first consequence vis-à-vis freedom.

In his essay "Non-reductive Physicalism," Rorty develops the image of the person as a "network which reweaves itself," rather than a network that is rewoven by a distinct agent.[42] As Martin Hollis has argued, there is no room for active choice in this model, because the person as a whole network is always merely responding to outside stimuli.[43] There is no 'self' apart from this network. 'Self', according to Rorty, is a term that the unlearned use to describe this network, but it does not represent anything that is separate from the network, just as there is no 'I' that picks and chooses its own beliefs and desires.[44] Rorty's concern here is to move away from a Cartesian dualism, but he moves so far that the only way left to describe the human person is as a being who is, to use Hollis's apt phrase, "relentlessly passive."[45]

The upshot of this relentless passivity is that there is no room for active creativity, for self-interpretation, for understanding oneself to be an 'I' with any lively sense of personal freedom.[46] Freedom of this kind, along with moral responsibility, has been cast into what Rorty calls a "pre-philosophical" category.[47] But the philosophical move fails, because the one creative task Rorty allows the human person is redescription of one's past.[48] The point of this redescription is self-interpretation[49] and self-judgment.[50] Yet, as Hollis points out, Rorty needs a concept of an 'I' for his overall project to make sense, because relentlessly passive beings cannot be "active self-interpreters."[51]

Yet since Rorty insists that there is no self, that there is nothing to the idea of an 'I', there is for him no possibility for genuine human freedom. What we come to think of as our self is just what we have internalized from our finite and contingent existence. We lack the freedom of self-creation, the ultimate freedom of self-disposition. We are our experience, our histories, and the only creativity we have is retrospective as we redescribe our histories in reweaving our stories. Prospective creativity is not completely ruled out, but it is certainly compromised, because the construal of a 'self' beyond the present is called into question. For example, if I am, in my totality, what happens to me, then I claim continuity with my past selves on the bases of history, but how can I project my present self onto some future self? As Charles Taylor points out, we need "something like an a priori unity of a human life through its whole extent," or something close to this, to make sense of our whole lives.[52]

Contingency

The second consequence of viewing ourselves as internalizations of the external is that we are utterly vulnerable to contingency. When Rorty says that we are socially constructed all the way down, he is saying that we are contingent and finite through and through, in our entirety products of 'external' factors, including our bodies. He wants us to abandon all efforts at transcendence, all attempts to see our existence in any context larger than our constructed selves.[53] This is what acceptance of our contingency involves for him. But we need to consider here his concept of contingency. For Rorty, contingency means nonnecessity, such that there is no overall design or essence causing certain features or claims to be true about human persons. But it also involves for him a total vulnerability to what happens to us. Consequently, his understanding of contingency lacks genuine uncertainty, a notion traditionally associated with contingency. The result is that Rortian contingency implies predictability. Recall that Rorty's attempt to do justice to the experience of being caused is set in a framework that sees causes and effects as indistinguishable links in a single chain. This means that the fact that we cannot predict behaviors way into the future is due to our lack of full knowledge of all present conditions. In *Philosophy and the Mirror of Nature*, Rorty denies explicitly that "anything is in principle unpredictable."[54] In practice, of course, even if we had full knowledge of present conditions we would not engage in making these predictions "except as an occasional pedagogical exercise."[55] Thus, Rorty's view of contingency leaves no room for freedom to disrupt the chain of cause and effect and thereby make life in principle unpredictable. The human person, then, is finite and contingent through and through, relentlessly passive and unfree. This does not, however, mean that there is no novelty or newness to life, or that life is experienced as passive and predictable. Novelty itself can enrich our lived experience, even if it is now understood to arise because of idiosyncratic events in life. In *Contingency, Irony, and Solidarity*, Rorty observes, "It hardly matters how the trick was done."[56] His point is that we cling to the idea of a self as the source of novelty, as the center from which we generate new and surprising elements in our lives. He wants us to see that viewing the 'self' in a mechanistic, determined way does not entail sacrificing the qualities of experience that delight and enrich us. Moreover, changing our perspective here frees us from always searching for meaning that connects our inner selves with something beyond us.

Dialogue

So what might Rahner and Rorty, speaking from such different viewpoints, say to one another that might point us in the direction of understanding the human person and freedom anew? There are three insights from Rorty's underlying anthropology and his pragmatist project on the whole that challenge Rahner's thought, or at least challenge the ideas about personhood and freedom to which Rahner's thought easily lends itself. The first is that we have an essential self. A pragmatist critique such as Rorty's calls attention to the way that Rahner's anthropology lends itself to a too easy essentialism. If we look at what Rahner himself has to say on the subject, we find that he is squarely in line with Thomas Aquinas's metaphysics of being.[57] Rahner does not see us as having an essence that is in any way separable from our existence, at least not during our lifetime. Our being is an intrinsically interrelated essence and existence that is separable only conceptually. The problem arises because Rahner expresses much of this in a conceptual rubric developed by Immanuel Kant, who does see a separableness to our noumenal and phenomenal selves that is at least more epistemologically significant than Rahner's view. For Kant, the only way we can know of our transcendent, noumenal self is through logical deduction, whereas Rahner seeks precisely here to go beyond Kant. While Kant identifies knowledge of God, immortality, and freedom through logical deduction, his famous three postulates of practical reason,[58] Rahner argues that we have built into our beings the capacity to know something of God, to experience freedom, and to understand ourselves to be eternal.[59]

The second pragmatist critique is directly related: the very idea that we have genuine, creative freedom. Bearing in mind the Kantian view of freedom as existing only on the noumenal level, it would be possible to respond to a pragmatist critique of Rahner's view of human freedom as a misconstrual of Rahner's metaphysics as strictly Kantian. One could point to Rahner's notion of freedom as a unity comprising mediated and unmediated, or transcendental, freedom as distinct from Kant's postulate that freedom exists in the noumenal realm.[60] But that would miss the problem that the pragmatist brings to our attention. That is the move that Kant makes to account for freedom as coexisting with mechanistic determinism. The pragmatist Rorty drops freedom altogether, accepting mechanism as a welcome decentering of self,[61] but Rahner follows Kant in assuming mechanistic determinism as the overarching worldview in relation to which freedom must be understood.

When Kant developed his theory of freedom as transcendent, existing in the noumenal realm, he did so to save the idea of freedom from Newton's mechanistic determinism. Kant accepted the view that the physical world is a world of cause and effect that allows for the reliable prediction of outcomes if all initial causes are known. The physical world is what Kant terms the phenomenal.[62] On his view, mechanistic determinism does indeed hold in the phenomenal realm, explaining why we experience outside factors as causing events to happen. What mechanistic determinism could not explain, however, was our sense of obligation to the moral law, to act out of duty, and to be self-legislators. Mechanistic determinism also could not account for human dignity or for the capacity to be autonomous and responsible.[63] Only the postulation of freedom in the unknowable but deducible noumenal realm could account for these features of existence.

To argue that Rahner takes us beyond the Kantian postulate with respect to freedom, then, is not to go far enough, because the real difficulty is that Rahner is still attempting to account for existential freedom as coexisting with a mechanistic worldview. This is just the worldview that has been discredited since early in the twentieth century, at least on the quantum level, with evidence against it on the biological and systematic levels as well. To move forward to the point where we can discuss freedom meaningfully, then, we have to move past Newton, not just Kant. When we do so in the final section, we will see that Rahner's anthropology is still capable of providing important grounding for Christian ethics, but it can do so only if his idea of human freedom is treated metaphorically to reflect the new scientific view. Moving past Newton, however, is hardly the pragmatist solution. As noted above, the pragmatist idea is to accept mechanistic determinism and let freedom go altogether. So although the pragmatist view prompts us to question Rahner's articulation of freedom in Kantian terms, it does not require us to accept its solution.

A third critique that Rorty could make of Rahner is that we do experience ourselves to be caught in tides of cause and effect to a sometimes overwhelming degree. The pragmatist embrace of mechanism offers a way of capturing this facet of existence. Rahner can articulate an account of freedom as knowable through experience, but he clearly does not do justice to the degree to which we also experience ourselves as caused not just by God, but also by the more mundane aspects of existence that appear to be entirely out of our control. Who we are today is not just the result of how we have used our freedom. Rahner sees this, of course, but his construal of humans as deeply free makes it too easy to lose sight of the degree of causation in life. Rorty's view of contingency may be too expansive, obliterating freedom as it does, but it calls our attention to the fact that even interpretations that lend themselves to essentialist readings are suspect because they risk missing the depth of our vulnerability to what is outside ourselves.

If we turn to ask what Rahner could say to Rorty by way of critique, we again find that responses to Kant and ultimately Newton lurk in the background. Rahner's account, in providing a compelling reason to *care* about human contingency, can be seen as an implicit critique of views such as Rorty's that offer no such compelling reason to care.[64] Human beings may be radically affected by what happens to them, and the pragmatist sees this, but the significance of this aspect of existence itself depends on our view of human beings. If we care only about human persons, those beings whom 'we', the socially powerful, have decided to count as persons, then we can restrict our care to the effects of contingency on only those persons. This, of course, is exactly the opposite of what Rorty wants to happen. He hopes that we will decide to see more and more human beings as like ourselves. But he cannot help but run the risk that we will see fewer and, if we do, his approach generates no internal self-critique. If, however, we agree with Rahner and see all human beings as possessing an independent value by virtue of their capacity for selfhood, freedom, and responsible action, then we need to care about the effects of contingency on all human beings. This gives us a much stronger warrant for ethical analysis. Although Rahner deepens Kant's insights on these aspects of human existence, it is clearly Kant's basic articulation that Rahner uses to render his moral realism regarding the moral value of each human being, and recognition of this independent value is rejected in Rorty's underlying anthropology. Opposing Kant, Rorty sees human dignity and treating others decently as unrelated. In his estimation, only those who think they need a reason to treat others well will want to view human dignity as an attribute that requires a certain kind of treatment.[65]

Rahner's account also challenges Rorty's in that Rahner's takes human experience of selfhood and freedom more seriously. Rorty sees these as tired metaphors that the unlearned may continue to use, but only out of ignorance. In fact, he welcomes mechanism precisely because it counters notions of a 'true self' that is independent of its causes.[66] Rorty focuses on the experience of causality in his conception of contingency, but he largely ignores the experience of noncausality. Thus, as Hollis and others have noted, in this respect Rorty's pragmatist account does not do justice to life as we live it. However, if we look closely at what Rahner might say to Rorty here, it is that the entire *idea* of transcendence is rejected. For Rahner, intrinsic human value derives in part from what he calls our transcendent nature, and mediated freedom is impossible to construe apart from transcendent, unmediated freedom. Once again, to understand Rorty's rejection of these concepts, we must see it in terms of the Kantian response to a Newtonian worldview. In these terms, when Rorty rejects the *idea* of transcendence, he rejects Kant's metaphysical anthropology and moral realism. However, he does not reject what Kant accepts at the phenomenal level: the Newtonian worldview. He nuances it, yes, as nonreductive physicalism, but by and large he accepts it. He asserts that the dichotomy between freedom and mechanism is misplaced, but he lets go of anything like genuine freedom in favor of mechanism.[67] At times he gestures toward a kind of compatabilist view that sees creativity as coexisting with determinism, but he clearly sides with mechanism over noncausality. On the whole, causality is too privileged in Rorty's account because, as is discussed below, noncausality also has its place. By wholeheartedly embracing mechanism as a healthy decentering of the human 'self', Rorty has no room to accommodate the noncausality that science now validates.

This means that Rorty's pragmatism, like Rahner's anthropology, is flawed by the assumption of a Newtonian worldview, at least as the scientific framework for considering the human person.[68] This assumption of mechanistic determinism has been dominant in Western religious and philosophical thought since Newton. That it so affects the views of thinkers of the stature of Rahner and Rorty, thinkers who otherwise stand out for their serious engagement of science,[69] suggests that a move beyond this scientifically outdated worldview is in order, because this move holds the promise of resolving some of the difficulties regarding human personhood and freedom created by that framework. To an exploration of this possibility we now turn.

Freedom and Personhood in a New Paradigm

Since the early part of the twentieth century, scientists working at the subatomic level of nature have had to grapple with an intractable indeterminacy that is formally capsuled in what is known as the Heisenberg uncertainty principle. Christopher Mooney, in his brilliant chapter on the significance of this principle in *Theology and Scientific Knowledge*, puts the principle this way: "the more accurately one knows by repeated experiment the position of any subatomic particle, the less accurately one knows its momentum, and vice versa. The quantum state of a subatomic particle (its position and momentum) can thus never be known or predicted with certainty."[70] Initially, one might ask, What has the activity of subatomic particles to do with questions of human personhood and specifically human freedom? After all, this indeterminacy has been subject to long debate in the scientific community. Moreover, consensus among quantum physicists that this indeterminacy is truly ontological rather than epistemological has emerged only recently.[71] And even if one accepts this indeterminacy as ontological at the quantum level of existence, one has to ask whether or not Newtonian determinacy holds in the visible world of physical existence.

As Mooney himself observes, physicists were long happy to accept the implications of the uncertainty principle for quantum analysis without connecting them to their views of the world of nature on the whole.[72] It seemed that there was a significant disjuncture between subatomic nature, what Mooney refers to as the "microworld," and the visible, "macroworld."[73] This was thought to be due to the sheer difference in size: the indeterminacy was so small in magnitude that it faded to zero for all practical purposes at the macro level, and thus Newtonian causation held for all but the subatomic level.[74] However, it turns out that this is not the case, with few exceptions. The norm is now more one of in-principled uncertainty, not perfect predictability. As Mooney puts it, "almost all complex dynamic systems are recognized as unstable."[75] Instability here does not imply disorder, necessarily, just uncertainty. Over time, over large numbers, a kind of order emerges in processes in nature, but one cannot say with certainty in advance what this order will be or how long it will last. This "structured chaos," Mooney tells us, is the subject of chaos theory, which "has already placed complex systems beyond the grip of any mechanistic determinism."[76] It has done so because, as Ivars Peterson has observed, "[s]omehow predictability and unpredictability together reside in the same set of equations."[77] Certain predictability is no longer the primary assumption or goal of scientific inquiry at the systematic level as well.

Another interesting example, though not fully confirmed yet, is emerging from the Human Genome Project. A week after the formal report of data for the project revealed the startling likelihood that human beings possess between 30,000 and 40,000 genes, approximately 100,000 fewer than expected,

Stephen Jay Gould called the discovery monumental in a *New York Times* editorial. Scientists had expected the larger number to account for the complexity of the human body, estimating that since approximately 140,000 specific genetic signals were required for this complexity, approximately 140,000 genes must exist, each one sending one signal. Gould describes the significance of the discovery this way: "Human complexity cannot be generated by 30,000 genes under the old view of life embodied in what geneticists literally called . . . their 'central dogma': . . . [that there existed] one direction of causal flow from code of message to assembly of substance." He later observes, "But the deepest ramifications will be scientific or philosophical in the largest sense. From its late 17th century inception in modern form, science has strongly privileged the reductionist mode of thought that breaks overt complexity into constituent parts and then tries to explain the totality by the properties of these parts and simple interactions fully predictable from the parts." It seems that the assumption of full predictability has fallen in the macroworld as well.[78] It is of note that the lower than expected estimate is not fully established. In July 2001, a team of scientists from Ohio developed a genomic map that estimated the number of genes to be between 65,000 and 75,000: much larger than the initial report, but still only half of the expected amount.[79] While no definitive answer has yet emerged as to the number of genes, it nonetheless appears that it will be far below the expected amount, suggesting that Gould's observations remain valid.

The importance of all of this for ethics is that the macroworld, including the world of human behavior, is best described as a world in which all 'predictions' must be in the modest form of probabilities, just as they are in the microworld. At the subatomic level, one can only speak of the probability of a given particle having a particular location and velocity.[80] In the macroworld, it may be possible to make predictions with a high probability of accuracy, but it is no longer possible to think in terms of absolute certainty or direct, unassailable causality. Thus, the connection between the two levels of existence may not be strictly physicalist, but it is at least one of analogy. Significantly, this connection means that the scientific paradigm itself cannot be used to rule out the possibility of freedom and, even more, it provides enough theoretical space to think about human freedom as real and not as an illusion of experience. This is a seminal advance for ethics. Samuel Johnson's memorable phrase regarding freedom, that "[a]ll theory is against it, all experience for it,"[81] now needs to be updated. The compelling and abiding human experience of freedom has some theory that is for it.

Of course, the existence of noncausality does not prove that humans have direct control over it and thus does not prove the existence of genuine human freedom in the rigorous sense. It does, however, mean that scientific theory can no longer be used to rule it out completely. If Harvard anthropologist Daniel Lieberman is correct that in terms of science one must operate with something less than confidence in having the "complete truth" because "[o]ne can only look for what, at a given time, cannot be proven wrong,"[82] then the existence of human freedom has at least a minimal claim to scientific respect. The existence of noncausality, in other words, opens a crack in the mechanistic determinism of Newton's worldview such that it now makes theoretical sense to speak of human freedom without resorting to a separate level of existence, such as Kant's noumenal realm. It thereby also offers a way of making sense of common human observations, such as the fact that while sociologists and psychologists can note trends in behavior patterns based on early experiences in life, no one can say with certainty that a particular kind of background or experience will lead necessarily to a particular kind of behavior later in life. This degree of uncertainty in prediction might have until recently been regarded as a mere epistemological failure, as Rorty's position suggests, but it is now seen to be an ineluctable feature of human existence, a feature that can be described well by the word 'freedom'.

Even more support for the theoretical grounding of freedom can be found in the description of human beings as finite and contingent given in chapter 1. The idea that genuine human freedom exists can be generated in terms of the fundamental conditions of existence. This move does not by itself demonstrate fully that human freedom exists, but it offers a way of seeing a space for human freedom that is entirely consistent with the non-Newtonian scientific worldview.

In chapter 1, limitation and dependency are offered as the primary and best explicators of finitude and contingency, respectively. Moreover, to recapitulate a point made there, we are not merely beings who experience limitation and dependency to some degree at all levels of existence. Instead, we are beings who experience synergistically our limitation and dependency. That is, we are beings who are contingently finite and finitely contingent and thus we experience our finitude as itself contingent and our contingency as itself limited.

Saying that our finitude is contingent is saying that the ways in which we are limited depend on factors outside of ourselves at each moment.[83] For example, the limitations that define our specific abilities are contingent upon our genetic makeup (and thus upon our parents), the time in which we live, the people that we meet, the resources that are available to us, and so forth. We are not the instantiation of pure limitation, but particular beings with very specific ways of being limited and experiencing limitation in this world.

Through our experience of these contingent limitations, we come to recognize the limitation of existence, but we do not experience pure limitation or even genuinely random limitations.

Likewise, our contingency is limited. We do not experience all possible ways of being dependent in the world. We only experience our own particular ways and the ways in which we might observe others as dependent. Thus I am dependent upon my parents for my genetic makeup, but not upon all parents. I get only one set of genes, one particular location in time, one lifetime of experiences, all of which I am dependent upon, but each of which is ultimately limited.

There is one more way in which we experience finite contingency, and this is the way that creates the place for freedom: Our dependency as a feature of created existence is itself limited.[84] Were it not limited, we would be wholly determined by it. Recall the view of the human person offered by Richard Rorty. It is a view of the human person as contingent all the way down: as unlimited contingency. Rorty thus quite consistently finds no room for genuine freedom.[85] But the understanding of the conditions of existence offered here has a different kind of consistency, for it maintains that our finitude is contingent and our contingency is finite. The myriad ways in which we are dependent are part of existence and so characterized by limitation. Our contingency does not go all the way down. It, too, is limited and this limitation creates the space for freedom.

The existence of indeterminism in a non-Newtonian worldview and the philosophical coherence of freedom with an understanding of human persons as finitely contingent and contingently finite comprise the beginnings of a cumulative case for the existence of genuine human freedom. While they do not and cannot prove human freedom's existence in a rigorous sense, they shift the balance toward a view of human persons as genuinely free, a view, moreover, that supports the abiding human experience of freedom. This view, especially the implications of a non-Newtonian worldview, indicate that both the pragmatist assumptions about the human person as exemplified by Rorty's account[86] and a metaphysically articulated theological anthropology such as Rahner's stand in need of modification. Consider the pragmatist case first. Rorty's idea that the human person is socially constructed through and through might still hold a functional value, because it does call attention to our experience of causality and it does critique our proclivity to essentialize whatever qualities we find desirable at a given place and time, but Rorty's view needs to be enhanced with an account of the in-principled unpredictability of human existence. Rorty does at times leave a place for chance in his account, for example, when he suggests that "abnormal discourse" might be generated "as the sparks fly upward,"[87] but he makes it clear elsewhere that chance, like novelty, is not generated freely. It is experienced as chance because it is unexpected. Its cause strikes us as idiosyncratic, but that is because of its unexpectedness or its rarity, not any inherent unpredictability.[88] Leaving a place for this kind of chance, therefore, does not challenge his exclusion of freedom. If, however, he were to provide a richer account of chance as arising freely, and not just as arising with an unknown cause, his concept of contingency as entailing certain predictability in principle would have to go. Predictability, again, could only be spoken of in terms of probabilities. At the very least, then, the pragmatist account given by Rorty would have to be modified to show a deeper appreciation of human vulnerability to what is in principle unknowable.

But this is the least that is indicated. A move away from Newtonian causation also calls into serious question Rorty's relegation of questions concerning human freedom to the prephilosophical category.[89] Given the theoretical space opened up for freedom, it is clear that the question of human freedom belongs in the philosophical realm. Rorty's anthropology, then, stands as an important critique to a long tradition of convenient essentializations and, most significantly here, as a reminder that however important the place of indeterminism is for understanding the human person, a deep appreciation of the contingency and vulnerability of human existence must be retained.

For Rahner, the implications suggest different modifications.[90] The most important is that his use of the term "transcendental" has to be severed from its Kantian and thus Newtonian links. In particular, "transcendental freedom" needs to be understood as a metaphorical way of referring to the fundamental element of noncausality. Particularly when this noncausality is viewed in terms of the new scientific view as the existence of multiple potentialities,[91] it is appropriate to use transcendental freedom as a descriptive metaphor. In the scientific paradigm, what we observe as reality is the result of a particular potentiality being actualized. This meshes well with Rahner's view that transcendental freedom grounds mediated freedom. Metaphorically, then, one could describe an act of freedom as the choosing of one potentiality over others, the result of which, in Rahnerian terms, is seen as the result of "mediated freedom." Treating "transcendental freedom" as metaphor, then, describes the newly apparent fact that noncausality is an element of existence that provides the condition for the possibility of free choice. But because it is understood metaphorically, there is the implicit acknowledgment that there may be more to this element of noncausality than "transcendental freedom" conveys. Thus, an appropriate degree of epistemic humility is built into the concept.

Once this move is made to recast Rahner's account of transcendental freedom as a metaphor for indeterminism that provides theoretical grounds for freedom, then all of Rahner's ideas that depend on a view of the human person as free are similarly open to reinterpretation in a way that is reflective of the new scientific paradigm. Such an endeavor is beyond the scope of the present work, but it has the potential to keep his rich theological and ethical insights relevant as we move forward in this new century. We must do so, however, with the pragmatist critiques ever in mind.

Thus, while both Rorty and Rahner offer us much richness in their understandings of human existence, neither gives us a fully adequate anthropology because, in different ways, both their views are shaped by mechanistic determinism. As such, neither does justice to the non-Newtonian world as it is. Because the new scientific paradigm rejects mechanistic determinism as the best description of the world available in favor of a view that sees indeterminism as established in the very structure of nature, we need to develop a new concept of what it means to be human, and this concept needs to be one that is open to the idea of human freedom and is able to engage it theoretically. The view of the human person as finite and contingent generated in chapter 1, though it has deep affinities with the Rahnerian view, does not depend on the metaphysical structure that supports his. It is, however, fully open to seeing human persons as genuinely free, based on scientific and philosophical grounds, though it does so with the epistemic humility that a metaphoric reformulation of Rahner's transcendental freedom generates. That is, it accepts that it is enough for now to speak of indeterminacy as grounds for freedom without claiming to know all that indeterminacy might imply for human existence.

Yet if it is now possible to speak of human persons as genuinely free without clear scientific contradiction, the question that immediately arises is, How free? This is a crucial question for our understanding of what it means to be finite, contingent, and free, because the existence of human freedom intersects in a complex way with our vulnerability to the conditions of existence. On the one hand, it provides a limit to our vulnerability. Our conditions of existence give rise to and shape our possibilities, but they do not fully determine our choices. We do not exist in a strict system of cause and effect. So it is important to ask to what degree our freedom might give us control over the possibilities that arise for us. On the other hand, if as human persons we are free to exercise some control in relation to our possibilities, and these choices give rise to new possibilities for ourselves and others, then we are also vulnerable to our freedom. Freedom thus has the capacity to limit and intensify our vulnerability, and so an attempt to assess human freedom vis-à-vis vulnerability is needed for a more complete view of the human person. A turn to the moral luck debate crystallized by Thomas Nagel is now indicated for this assessment.

Notes

1. Immanuel Kant underscores the traditional importance of freedom to ethics in his preface to his *Groundwork of the Metaphysic of Morals*, when he notes that for the ancient Greeks the science of freedom was called ethics. Kant, *Groundwork of the Metaphysic of Morals*, trans. H. J. Paton (New York: Harper & Row, 1956), 55.

2. See Jeffrey Stout, *The Flight from Authority: Religion, Morality, and the Quest for Autonomy* (Notre Dame, Ind.: University of Notre Dame Press, 1981), 54–59, 269.

3. For a typology of possible relations of theology to science, and an argument for the type in which theological claims do not contradict science, see James Gustafson, *Ethics from a Theocentric Perspective, Vol. 1: Theology and Ethics* (Chicago: University of Chicago Press, 1981), 252–59.

4. Richard Rorty, *Objectivity, Relativism, and Truth* (New York: Cambridge University Press, 1991), 125. The view Rorty gestures toward seems to be of a compatabilist kind, where mechanism is not rejected but the possibility of occasions of (free?) creativity is still maintained.

5. Karl Rahner, *Foundations of Christian Faith*, trans. William V. Dych (New York: Crossroad, 1978), 7. Regarding Rahner's starting point, Anne Carr notes that for Rahner, anthropology leads to theology and theology leads to anthropology. However, she argues that Rahner's point of departure is always theological, because "[a] theological question is always at the heart of his work." Carr, *The Theological Method of Karl Rahner* (Missoula, Mont.: Scholars, 1977), 260. Rahner himself suggests that the two endeavors are mutually informative, in "The Dignity and Freedom of Man," in *Theological Investigations*, vol. 2, trans. Karl-H. Kruger (New York: Crossroad 1963), 241. In *Foundations*, he also makes the point that philosophy and theology are interconnected in anthropology (25). All of this implies that anthropology is not the only starting point for him, although it clearly is a valid intellectual starting point for him.

6. Rahner, *Foundations*, 11.

7. Rahner, *Foundations*, 11.

8. Anne Carr, "Starting with the Human," in *A World of Grace*, ed. Leo J. O' Donovan, 17–30 (New York: Crossroad, 1989), 19.

9. Rahner, *Foundations*, 25–26.

10. Rahner, *Foundations*, 27.

11. Rahner, *Foundations*, 29.

12. Rahner, *Foundations*, 29.

13. Rahner defines transcendental experience as "the subjective, unthematic, necessary and unfailing consciousness of the knowing subject that is co-present in

every spiritual act of knowledge, and the subject's openness to the unlimited expanse of all possible reality." Rahner, *Foundations*, 20.

14. Rahner, *Foundations*, 29.

15. Rahner, *Foundations*, 32.

16. Rahner, *Foundations*, 34.

17. Rahner, *Foundations*, 35.

18. Rahner, *Foundations*, 37.

19. Rahner, *Foundations*, 35.

20. Rahner, *Foundations*, 36.

21. Rahner, *Foundations*, 36.

22. Carr, "Starting with the Human," 27, points out the reciprocal nature of the relationship.

23. Rahner, *Foundations*, 40–41.

24. Rahner, *Foundations*, 42.

25. Rahner, *Foundations*, 44.

26. Charles Taylor, "Rorty in the Epistemological Tradition," in *Reading Rorty: Critical Responses to "Philosophy and the Mirror of Nature" (and Beyond)*, ed. Alan Malachowski (Cambridge, Mass.: Blackwell, 1990), 273.

27. Richard Rorty, *Contingency, Irony, and Solidarity* (New York: Cambridge University Press, 1989), 8.

28. Rorty, *Objectivity, Relativism, and Truth*, 13.

29. Rorty, *Philosophy and the Mirror of Nature* (Princeton, N.J.: Princeton University Press, 1979), 174.

30. Rorty, *Philosophy and the Mirror of Nature*, 360.

31. Rorty, *Philosophy and the Mirror of Nature*, 10.

32. Rorty, *Objectivity, Relativism, and Truth*, 14.

33. Rorty, *Contingency, Irony, and Solidarity*, xiii.

34. Rorty, *Philosophy and the Mirror of Nature*, 38.

35. Rorty, *Contingency, Irony, and Solidarity*, 91.

36. Rorty, *Contingency, Irony, and Solidarity*, 190.

37. Rorty, *Contingency, Irony, and Solidarity*, 192.

38. The benefit of the realist position over the pragmatist position is thus primarily retrospective. The moral realist can say that a given person or group was immorally deprived of full human rights, while the pragmatist can say only that the deprivation occurred according to the accepted terms of inclusion of the time.

39. Rorty, *Consequences of Pragmatism* (Minneapolis: University of Minnesota Press, 1982), xlii.

40. Rorty, *Contingency, Irony, and Solidarity*, 185.

41. Rorty, *Contingency, Irony, and Solidarity*, 8.

42. Martin Hollis, "The Poetics of Personhood," in *Reading Rorty*, 253. Hollis offers a penetrating critique of Rorty's passive notion of personhood.

43. Hollis, "Poetics of Personhood," 253.

44. Rorty, *Objectivity, Relativism, and Truth*, 123.

45. Hollis, "Poetics of Personhood," 253.

46. This passivity also calls into question his decisional view of the human person, because now our decisions are really the products of external factors and do not involve any active, personal choice on our part to include or exclude beings in the category of persons.

47. Rorty, *Philosophy and the Mirror of Nature*, 34–37.

48. Rorty, *Contingency, Irony, and Solidarity*, 97.

49. Rorty, *Contingency, Irony, and Solidarity*, 73.

50. Rorty, *Contingency, Irony, and Solidarity*, 97.

51. Hollis, "Poetics of Personhood," 253–54.

52. Charles Taylor, *Sources of the Self: The Making of the Modern Identity* (Cambridge, Mass.: Harvard University Press, 1989), 51.

53. Rorty nuances this view at the end of "Freud and Moral Reflection" when he advocates that we read narratives that help us "identify . . . with communal movements [and in doing so] engender a sense of being a machine geared into a large machine." Rorty, "Freud and Moral Reflection," in *Essays on Heidegger and Others* (New York: Cambridge University Press, 1991), 163. Here, we can connect with something larger than ourselves, but larger in size, not in magnitude or importance.

54. Rorty, *Philosophy and the Mirror of Nature*, 355.

55. Rorty, *Philosophy and the Mirror of Nature*, 354.

56. Rorty, *Contingency, Irony, and Solidarity*, 17.

57. See Thomas Aquinas, *Summa Theologica*, trans. Fathers of the Divine Dominican Province (Westminster, Md.: Christian Classics, 1948), I, 76, 5–7.

58. Kant, *Critique of Practical Reason*, trans. Lewis White Beck (New York: Macmillan, 1956), 137.

59. For an account of Rahner's extension of Kant's epistemology on these points, see Barrie A. Wilson, "The Possibility of Theology after Kant: An Examination of Karl Rahner's *Geist in Welt*," *Canadian Journal of Theology* 12, no. 4 (1966): 245–58, esp. 250.

60. Note the problem Kant has of explaining how our exercise of autonomy beyond disposition of the will affects the phenomenal realm. Gordon E. Michalson Jr. has addressed this difficulty in Kant's account of moral development (regeneration) in "God and Kant's Ethical Commonwealth," *Thomist* 65 (2001): 84–85.

61. Rorty, "Freud and Moral Reflection," 144–45.

62. Kant, 52–59, *Critique of Practical Reason* and *Prolegomena to Any Future Metaphysics*, rev. Paul Carus trans. (New York: Bobbs-Merrill, 1950), 61.

63. For example, regarding obligation, see Kant, *Groundwork*, 86–87.

64. For problems relating to generating this care from Rorty's account, see Joyce Kloc McClure, "The Contingency of Solidarity: A Pragmatic Critique of Richard Rorty's Philosophy," *Horizons* 28, no. 1 (Spring 2001): 40–49.

65. Rorty, "Freud and Moral Reflection," 162.

66. Rorty, "Freud and Moral Reflection," 153.

67. Rorty, *Objectivity, Relativism, and Truth*, 125.

68. Rorty has criticized Kant for drawing a line between science and morals, with science being "Newtonian physics" (quoted in Stout, *Flight from Authority*, 130), but he has not moved beyond Kant's basic scientific hurdle with respect to freedom.

69. Rahner, for example, grapples with genetic engineering in an overall open way in "The Experiment with Man," *Theological Investigations*, vol. 9, trans. Graham Harrison (New York: Herder and Herder, 1972), 205–24, while Rorty engages science, especially physics, throughout his corpus.

70. Christopher Mooney, *Theology and Scientific Knowledge* (Notre Dame, Ind.: University of Notre Dame Press, 1996), 83.

71. Mooney, *Theology and Scientific Knowledge*, 98.

72. Mooney, *Theology and Scientific Knowledge*, 88.

73. Mooney, *Theology and Scientific Knowledge*, 96, 100.

74. Mooney, *Theology and Scientific Knowledge*, 100.

75. Mooney, *Theology and Scientific Knowledge*, 100.

76. Mooney, *Theology and Scientific Knowledge*, 101.

77. Ivars Peterson, *The Mathematical Tourist* (New York: Freeman, 1988), 145.

78. Stephen Jay Gould, "Humbled by the Genome's Mysteries," *New York Times on the Web*, February 19, 2001, Opinion section.

79. Fred A. Wright et al., "A Draft Annotation and Overview of the Human Genome," *Genome Biology* 2, no. 7 (July 2001): 0025.1–0025.18.

80. Christopher Mooney, *Theology and Scientific Knowledge*, 84. Mooney writes, "We can give no complete retrospective explanation of what we have seen an individual particle do. Causality as such is not eliminated, because physical situations still depend on each other. But they do so probabilistically: all we have from the past is a range of potentialities for the future."

81. Quoted in Margaret Farley, *Personal Commitments: Beginning, Keeping, Changing* (New York: Harper and Row, 1986), 26.

82. Daniel E. Lieberman, "Upending the Expectations of Science," *New York Times on the Web*, July 14, 2002, Opinion section.

83. This includes our dependency on our own prior choices. As the consideration of finitude in chapter 1 shows, once a choice has been made, it is no longer in our control to remake it. At times, of course, we can make new choices that reverse the effects of prior choices, but this is not the same thing as remaking them, nor is it always possible.

84. This limitation of dependency refers to our dependency in relation to created existence. It does not rule out the possibility of total, radical dependency upon God for existence, provided that relationship allows for human freedom. Thomas Aquinas's position on human freedom vis-à-vis God's freedom is a case in point. See, Aquinas, *Summa Theologica*, I, 83, 1 ad 3.

85. Rorty wants to consign the question of personal freedom to a prephilosophical realm, but clearly articulates a fully deterministic view of human action in *Philosophy and the Mirror of Nature* and elsewhere. See especially *Philosophy and the Mirror of Nature*, 34–47.

86.　It is more precise with Rorty to refer to this simply as a mechanistic worldview, not a Newtonian mechanistic worldview, since Rorty expressly identifies Freudian mechanism as an important development of Newton's view. See Rorty "Freud and Moral Reflection," 144–45.

87.　Rorty, *Philosophy and the Mirror of Nature*, 389.

88.　Rorty, *Essays on Heidegger and Others*, 152.

89.　Rorty, *Essays on Heidegger and Others*, 34–37.

90.　It is of interest here that Mooney chooses to develop the implications for Teilhard de Chardin's thought. The point, one that Mooney makes early on, is that all contemporary philosophy and theology must be reassessed in light of the new scientific paradigm. Mooney, *Theology and Scientific Knowledge*, 71–72.

91.　Mooney, *Theology and Scientific Knowledge*, 84.

CHAPTER THREE

Moral Luck and Vulnerability

$\mathcal{A}$s philosophers of the late twentieth century grappled with the ideas of human freedom and moral responsibility under the assumption of the Newtonian framework of mechanistic determinism, a category of thought developed to address this theoretical complex. This category is known as the moral luck debate. It stands in a long tradition of debate in Western philosophy and theology about human vulnerability to factors outside of our control, as well as the possibility of invulnerability to such factors. For example, the Platonic search for pure form is a search for that which transcends temporal vulnerability.[1] Boethian virtue provides a certainty about eternal happiness that is not vulnerable to the contingencies of the world.[2] The Christian notion of inner goodness, crystallized in the Kantian conception of the good will that is invulnerable to contingency, is a more modern example of the same.[3] Likewise, strong doctrines of particular Providence[4] and Predestination[5] offer protection against contingency.

Along with these endeavors to find or mark off a safe zone of invulnerability have been recognitions of vulnerability. Indeed, as Martha Nussbaum observes in *The Fragility of Goodness*, Plato's quest for the invulnerable demonstrates that he has a keen sense of the vulnerable, so keen that only a "radical solution" will do.[6] Aristotle did not believe that goodness could offer complete protection against luck. However, he stopped short of total vulnerability. On his view, luck can make it impossible for a person to completely enjoy happiness (*eudamonia*), but it will not completely destroy a truly good person.[7] So when Bernard Williams coined the term 'moral luck'[8] and he and Thomas Nagel first used it in a 1976 symposium on the subject of whether or not the sphere of morality, and in particular the moral will, could offer an escape from contingency, a long-standing issue about invulnerability was placed in a specific debate. In the context of this debate, the invulnerability under question is derived from freedom in two respects: the freedom of the will to choose well and a mode of moral evaluation that holds people responsible only for what they freely choose to do, but not for factors that are beyond their knowledge or control. What moral luck as a concept suggests is that luck, understood as that which is beyond our control and upon which we are in some ways dependent,[9] enters the sphere of the moral and either causes us to choose ill or influences outcomes such that we are held responsible for something other than what we have chosen to do.[10]

In the first section of this chapter, the issue of moral luck will be considered primarily in relation to Thomas Nagel's groundbreaking essay, "Moral Luck." Because Nagel offers a comprehensive categorization of types of moral luck, this essay serves as an organizing vehicle for the topic as a whole and the questions it generates. Moreover, the bulk of the critical literature on the subject more directly engages Nagel's arguments than Williams's. This fact no doubt is related to the way that Williams's essay concerns agent self-evaluation, while Nagel's deals more with moral evaluation of both self and others. This section concludes that, while Nagel does make dramatically clear the fact that luck impinges deeply on the lives that we lead, he engages the entire issue from a quasi-Kantian point of view. He articulates the debate in Kantian terms and clearly accepts as did Kant the idea of causal determinism in the phenomenal world. However, while he wants to hang on to notions of freedom and moral responsibility, he simply says that we must do so because it is important to our sense of what it means to be a human being. Unfortunately, his work is flawed by his failure to offer a theoretical argument for the existence of freedom. Because he articulates the debate in Kantian terms, he does not question Kant's assumption of mechanistic determinism. The scientific developments of the twentieth century that suggest a plausible theoretical grounding of freedom and hence the possibility of free will even in the face of deep vulnerability to finitude and contingency are left out of the debate. He focuses on evaluation of actions and clings to the ideas of human freedom and responsibility without providing an account for freedom that would justify this move. Such a weak appeal to freedom and responsibility does little to resolve the question of moral luck. Alternatively, if one accepts the new scientific worldview, then it is harder to demonstrate the existence of genuine moral luck, because one cannot ignore the possibility of free choice, even in the face of deep vulnerability to luck. However, it is likewise difficult to specify the degree of vulnerability to luck. Thus, while the theoretical space for freedom opened up by the new scientific paradigm provides a grounding for moral responsibility and challenges the notion that moral luck is total, the fact that the precise degree of vulnerability cannot be determined suggests that assessing moral responsibility, while an important part of ethical inquiry, is not the proper primary task. We get closer to the primary task if we seek to answer the question, What can it mean for us, with some capacity for freedom, to live lives that are deeply but not wholly vulnerable to contingency and finitude as conditions of existence? This new focus requires a new approach to ethics, one that redirects us from moral judgment and assignment of responsibility to discernment and acceptance. In the second section, a sketch is offered of this alternative approach to ethics. This sketch, in turn, leads into the work of part II of this book.

Moral Luck: The Issue

To have a particular view of the human person is already to have somewhat of a view of moral luck, and vice versa. Nagel himself notes the connection when he says, "What . . . do we have in mind that a person must *be* to be the object of these moral attitudes?"[11] But to start with familiar ground, consider Richard Rorty's pragmatist anthropology, which we have seen in chapter 2. For someone like Rorty, who holds that we are completely contingent and thus utterly vulnerable to the conditions of our existence, there is no point in talking about genuine human freedom because we are all utterly passive, living dependent lives that could be predicted had we the time and inclination to conduct what he refers to as the pedagogical exercise of prediction.[12] On Rorty's view, contingency accounts for the whole of human existence. By making this much of contingency, however, Rorty may actually make too little of it. Total dependency at the heart of human existence would matter little. If we were all sociobiological beings living caused and predictable lives, we would be merely going through the motions of existence.[13] Since everything that happened in our lives would be caused by external factors, we would attach no special importance to experiencing things as being beyond our control. Questions concerning human agency, and in particular the poignant question of moral luck, might be part of ordinary discourse, but they would serve no authentic purpose because they all address some notion of an active self, not the passive 'self' that Rorty sees.[14]

Rorty himself explicitly identifies moral luck as one of those questions that it is not profitable for us to pursue. He sees the topic as part of the legacy of Western philosophy. The fact that we still engage it says something about us and our history, but nothing in particular about essential aspects of human beings.[15] While Rorty does not explain his position on moral luck in depth, it is clear that his assessment follows directly from his anthropology. For 'moral luck' to make sense logically as a topic, one has to have some appreciation for the pinch it seeks to capture: that one can be held morally responsible for that which one was not free to choose or control. The pinch comes only because the assignment of moral responsibility assumes that we are free to choose and control, yet it appears that we can be held responsible when factors outside of our control affect moral evaluation. If there is no sense of the self as an active agent and thus no genuine freedom, there is nothing to give rise to a notion of moral evaluation in Nagel's sense. Everything might have a cause, but not a morally relevant cause. Given Rorty's view of the human person, moral luck is indeed a useless topic.

Thomas Nagel, however, engages the topic because, while he goes a long way toward adopting Rorty's depiction of the self as passive, he is unwilling to jettison completely the view that there is something unique about being human that requires some notion of personal responsibility. In his essay, "Moral Luck,"[16] he offers an expansive view of moral luck as a challenge to the Kantian view of the invulnerability of the good will and thus to notions associated with contemporary morality, such as moral responsibility. Nagel identifies four basic kinds of moral luck and finds that each one compromises the invulnerability of the good will, so that in the end, as he acknowledges, the area for responsibility and genuine human agency shrinks to the vanishing point and the self shrinks with it.[17] Rather than make the Rortian move of abandoning the question, however, Nagel insists that there is still something to the notion of a self that we cannot relinquish. Although he cannot offer a theoretical account of a genuine self, he maintains that we must continue to think of human persons as possessing an active self.

It is important to see just what Nagel is doing here. His analysis of moral luck convinces him that we continue to hold ourselves and one another morally responsible for factors that are outside our control, and yet we are not mistaken to do this. That we do so shows how important it is to being human to think of ourselves as responsible and free. Rorty identifies this move on Nagel's part as an instance of his "intuitive realism."[18] He describes Nagel's intuition that there is something important about retaining a notion of an active self as "drawing a line around a vacant place in the middle of the web of words, and then claiming that there is something there rather than nothing."[19] Rorty is right. Nagel wants to say that there is something distinct to being a human person, just as there is to being a bat and so forth.[20] Unfortunately, like Rorty has done with contingency, Nagel has developed such an expansive notion of moral luck that there simply is no way to account for human freedom and the self.

Rorty may be right about Nagel's move to hold on to a self, but it is Nagel who is right in trying to accommodate his intuition. He intuits the self, the feeling of agency, that is true to experience. But as interesting as Nagel's move may be with its forthrightness, it is unsatisfactory for the same reason that the anthropologies considered in chapter 2 are: the assumption of a Newtonian worldview. Nagel wants to challenge and discredit the Kantian view of morality as providing a degree of moral invulnerability, but he does so without questioning Kant's own assumption of mechanistic determinism. Given the prominence of Nagel's position on moral luck, and the comprehensiveness with which he lays out the issue, it is important to examine what he says in order to gain somewhat different insights than he intended, in light of the new scientific worldview presented in chapter 2.

Nagel's famous essay is thoroughly rooted in Kant's worldview. He begins his essay with a quotation from Kant in which Kant reifies the good will as something that "sparkles like a jewel."[21] For Kant, the gem-like quality of the good will rests in its independence from uncertain factors such as consequences to one's own actions and the actions of others. In his famous essay "On a Supposed Right to Lie from Altruistic Motives," Kant makes it clear that it is precisely the uncertainty that attaches to consequences that makes them unsuitable as justifications for moral action. The duty to tell the truth is a formal duty applying to everyone, regardless of the consequences of a particular case. Thus, in his answer to the question of whether or not one should lie to a murderer seeking a friend who has hidden in one's home, Kant directly offers reliance upon obedience to the moral law within as the only *certain* way to avoid the contingencies associated with the unknown and unknowable.[22]

It is this certainty, that no matter how things turn out one still acts correctly from a moral point of view if one wills to act in accordance with the moral law within, that Nagel calls into question. He does so by first noting that we hold people responsible only for the aspects of their actions that are under their control and then arguing that much less is under our control than is apparent. All of the factors that impact our actions and their outcomes but that are not directly under our control are what Nagel refers to as luck.[23] Insofar as luck enters into our moral evaluations, it is moral luck. Since 'moral' refers to what is under our control and 'luck' refers to what is beyond our control, the term 'moral luck' is used to suggest a paradox at the heart of moral evaluation.[24]

Both Nagel and Bernard Williams explicitly use the moniker 'moral luck' to call into question contemporary moral evaluation. But they do not do so identically. Williams is concerned mainly with agent self-evaluation. His intention is to show that the moral sphere is completely vulnerable to luck because the way in which an agent evaluates her or his own actions is directly dependent upon factors outside her or his control. For Williams, the analysis shows that conventional morality is inherently mistaken in its assumption that outside factors are not directly involved in our explicitly moral judgments. The moral realm, rather than being immune to luck, is completely permeated by it. Thus, he refers to moral luck as an "oxymoron."[25] He favors a return to an Aristotelian-type conception of morality that does not focus on the will as the center of morality, much less claim complete invulnerability for the moral sphere.[26]

Nagel, for his part, refers to moral luck as "paradoxical."[27] Unlike the oxymoron, which involves a direct contradiction, a paradox involves an apparent contradiction that actually has a point of unity or truth.[28] Nagel argues that, while our dominant form of moral evaluation assumes the invulnerability of the good will to factors outside the agent's control, it also involves such factors in the moral evaluations actually made. Although in "Moral Luck" he but briefly suggests that the contradiction only appears when moral evaluation is looked at from two different perspectives, the external and the internal, the objective and the subjective, he elsewhere develops this position in detail.[29] What he means by the subjective viewpoint is that, from an internal perspective, when we consider our own actions, we think of ourselves as morally responsible agents who act with some degree of autonomy, even if we cannot give an objective account of this self. But objectively speaking, our acts are so permeated by luck that they can hardly be thought of as free and we can hardly assign moral responsibility to anything that anyone does. That we continue to do so argues for some validity to the subjective experience and for the paradoxical nature of agency and action because it accounts for something in our experience that is important to our understanding of what it means to be human. It is not that one side completely contradicts the other. It is, rather, that both sides are (paradoxically) true. At the heart of morality lies paradox, not contradiction.

The main focus of Nagel's essay, though, is on what he refers to as the objective sphere. In this sphere, where we judge others as well as ourselves, we need to look more closely at how luck enters into moral evaluation, even as we deny that it does. To call our attention to this invasion, Nagel identifies four kinds of luck that he says play a significant, even if sometimes indirect role in our moral evaluations. These are constitutive luck, luck in one's circumstances, luck in how one is determined by antecedent circumstances, and luck in how one's actions and projects turn out.[30]

Both constitutive luck and antecedent luck relate to character: the former refers to personal features such as temperament, while the latter refers to how one is shaped by previous choices. Luck in circumstances and luck in consequences both refer to matters of fortune. This categorization is no accident. Nagel is specifically addressing Kant's conception of the invulnerability of the good will. In the first paragraph of the first section of *Groundwork*, Kant states that the good will is invulnerable to "character" and "gifts of fortune." Features of character, such as temperament, can be used well or ill, Kant observes, so they are dependent upon the will, not the other way around. Regarding matters of fortune, Kant asserts that they affect happiness, but not goodness of will. Moreover, gifts of fortune can lead to misuse unless accompanied by a good will, so happiness also is dependent on a good will, rather than the reverse.[31]

With his four categories of luck, then, Nagel directly takes on the Kantian conception of morality. His goal is to show that, in spite of theoretical allegiance to a Kantian morality, moral evaluation in practice takes factors relating to character and fortune into account in a significant way. Much of the debate in the literature concerns whether or not Nagel succeeds in showing that each of these four kinds of luck in fact plays a role in moral evaluation. Indeed, such a determination must be made if any insight is to be gained as to the existence or extent of moral luck.

Moral Evaluation

There is, however, a perplexing and generally unacknowledged confusion at the very center of the question of moral luck that must be explored before the more specific task of analyzing the various kinds of luck can be profitable. That confusion has to do with the oft repeated phrase, "moral evaluation." The real confusion regarding moral evaluation is that there is no specificity as to what is meant by the term. Early in the essay, Nagel identifies the condition of agent control, which entails agent choice, as key to our moral judgments about ourselves and others. He then goes on to say that factors outside agent control, "what is not produced by a good or bad will, in Kant's phrase," actually are included in moral judgments.[32] This broader evaluation is what he means by the vague phrase, "ordinary conditions of moral judgment."[33] Unfortunately, he does not address whether or not these other factors are proper to moral evaluation. Instead, Nagel freely moves around a variety of types of evaluations as if they were all, unquestionably, moral.[34] Legal judgments are assumed equivalent to moral assessments. Social opinion is treated as having moral weight. Similarly, all types of responsibility are taken to be moral responsibility.[35] The result is that it is never clear to us what exactly is meant by moral evaluation, and the matter is further complicated by the fact that much of the literature merely picks up where Nagel leaves off, continuing the vagueness.

"Gifts of Fortune"

Luck in consequences. This confusion is most apparent in Nagel's discussion of luck in consequences. Three of Nagel's examples of this kind of luck are the difference between rescuing someone from a burning building and dropping someone during a rescue attempt; the difference between driving up onto an empty sidewalk while intoxicated and driving up onto a sidewalk while intoxicated and killing a pedestrian who steps into one's path; and the difference between punishments for attempted murder and for murder.[36] Regarding the first, Nagel merely asserts that there is a "morally significant difference" between the successful rescue attempt and the unsuccessful one.[37] However, it is not at all clear why Nagel is so confident that the difference can be described as morally significant. With no further information, it is impossible to conclude that the difference has moral significance. If we were to learn, for instance, that the rescuer had recklessly endangered the other person in the rescue attempt and, further, that a safe rescue was known to be moments away, then we would be able to consider the difference as having moral significance. But even here, the judgment would not be certain. A reckless, unnecessary attempt has no higher moral standing than a failed attempt, even if the person is somehow rescued.[38] Only the difference between a heroic but circumspect attempt and a reckless and unnecessary one has moral significance. Why? Because we do continue to make moral assessments on the lines indicated by Kant. We look to the *motive* of the actor. For Kant, the whole of moral evaluation rests in determining a person's motive: whether one acts from a motive of duty or from a motive that merely does not conflict with a motive of duty.[39] For an action to be moral on Kant's account, one needs to act *aus Pflicht*, from a motive of duty to the categorical imperative, and not merely *mit Pflicht*, in accordance with duty. While we in general do not adhere strictly to Kant's understanding of duty in making moral assessments, we do look to motive as the key element in such assessments.

The difficulty, long recognized, is that motive is an internal element of an act. Assessing another's motive is akin to reading that person's mind and heart. While one can often speculate with reasonable accuracy what a person's motive is, one cannot have any great assurance that in a particular instance one has speculated correctly. As Kant observes in *Groundwork*, moral evaluations concern not actions themselves, which we can see, but their "inner principles," which we cannot see.[40]

This point is even more obvious in Nagel's second example. Nagel infers directly from the difference in the legal consequences to the two intoxicated drivers that there is a moral difference between the two actions. As Nagel sets up the example, the two drivers are equally intoxicated.[41] One makes it home without incident, while the other kills a pedestrian. His point is that it is entirely a matter of luck that in one case no pedestrian appears and that in the other one does. The former is then guilty of driving while intoxicated, while the latter is guilty of that as well as killing an innocent pedestrian and is liable to prosecution for manslaughter. Nagel's conclusion is that there is a morally significant difference between the two acts that can only be accounted for on the basis of luck, that is, moral luck. The same point holds for the third example cited, that of the difference in penalties for murder and attempted murder. The legal distinction is taken as a moral distinction.

One must ask here why Nagel is so sure that the moral assessment is identical with the legal determination. Nagel assumes that we will immediately see that there is a moral difference in the way the actions are evaluated, even though the information we have tells us that the actions were the same from the agents' perspectives. This, however, is not the only way one can look at the case. For example, it is entirely possible to say that morally speaking the agents' acts deserve the same evaluation, but legally speaking they do not.[42]

Legal judgments are not made as moral judgments *per se*, even though people may wish that they were. Joel Feinberg, the noted legal scholar, decries the difference in punishment based on outcomes, but he does so as one who has taken "a reformist position," advocating that "the severity of punishment be proportional to the moral blameworthiness of the offense."[43] That he advocates a *change* to this asymmetry shows that legal and moral judgments are not identical in current practice. Nagel's assumption that they are, and that we will recognize the symmetry, is mistaken.

The most basic reason that differences persist between moral and legal evaluations is that while moral evaluations are made on the basis of what is internal and unseen, as Kant noted, legal evaluations must proceed on the basis of what can be seen. Our legal system punishes on the basis of intent, what specifically the agent was trying to accomplish, or indeed accomplished, which can be reasonably inferred from the agent's action,[44] rather than on the basis of motive.[45] As a society, we have chosen to make our legal judgments on the only basis we can, what we can see or reasonably infer. We are, in this sense, consequentialists, Benthamites even, rather than Kantians. But when it comes to moral evaluations, we tend more toward Kant.[46]

Our legal system is actually more nuanced than this suggests. It is possible to identify four theoretical bases to punishment: retribution; rehabilitation; deterrence; and compensation.[47] Hegel, for example, most notably favored retribution, but a retribution that was restorative of right (by the "annulling of crime") for both society and the criminal.[48] Consequentialists tend to support the other three. Bentham, the preeminent consequentialist, advocated punishment principally for its value as a deterrent.[49] Whatever theory of punishment appeals most, however, is not the point so much as that we have a variety of factors that are not purely moral at work in determining how particular acts are punished. Take again Nagel's case of the two intoxicated drivers. Society punishes the two differently perhaps for a number of reasons, the primary one being that a greater harm is done in one case than the other. While one may disagree with society's approach in this matter, one cannot simply claim a moral difference where it does not exist. In treating legal judgments as identical to and indicative of moral judgments, Nagel is implying that the moral sphere is coextensive with the legal sphere, and that is simply not the case. Since this connection is Nagel's main ground for finding luck in consequences a case of moral luck, it is clear that Nagel has not proven his claim here.[50] What he has pointed to, unintentionally, is the far less weighty fact that our legal evaluations are not the same as our moral ones.

Luck in circumstances. Luck in one's circumstances, Nagel's other category of what Kant referred to as a gift of fortune, appears to be a more compelling candidate as a category of genuine moral luck. Here Nagel notes that our actions depend to some extent on the circumstances in which we find ourselves. Different circumstances give rise to different temptations and, possibly, actions. Nagel's example is the situation whereby some people were residents of Nazi Germany but most people were not. Those who lived in Nazi Germany were faced with a set of options most of us are never asked to face. He notes that many citizens of other countries would have engaged in the same atrocities German war criminals did had they been in the same circumstances. The fact that they did not, and so are not subject to the same condemnation, is for Nagel an example of moral luck.[51] Nagel treats this category briefly, using it to call attention to the fact that we do not have control over all of the opportunities we face for moral decision making. This is a case that, he says, shows that we are "morally at the mercy of fate" since "[w]e judge people for what they actually do or fail to do, not just for what they would have done if circumstances had been different."[52]

Nagel is right that luck plays an important part in the lives that we lead and the decisions that we must make. What must be determined is whether or not it makes a moral difference, or to what extent the difference made is moral. The case of the citizen of Nazi Germany is a powerful one, for it calls our attention to the possibility that some, if not most, of us generally face relatively easy choices about how to live in society, while others face quite difficult ones. Many Germans participated in the Nazi effort quite willingly, but there were no doubt many others who had to decide whether to support or resist the Nazis, where resistance could have cost them their lives. Most of us do not have our lives hanging in the balance as we weigh our decisions. In all likelihood, we feel lucky that we do not when we realize that others did, and often did not choose well because of that fact. We will never know for certain how we would have acted had we faced the same circumstances, and we are grateful if we never do know.

Again, however, the key issue that must be determined is whether or not the luck is moral luck, and that can only be determined based on some clarification of what is moral. Early in his essay, Nagel sets the terms of the debate when he says that agent control is key to the "ordinary conditions of moral judgment."[53] He goes on to say that in practice we tend to judge people morally for factors beyond their control: hence, moral luck. However, rather than concluding that moral luck exists, it is also possible to say that we simply are not careful enough in our moral judgments or in what we are willing to think of as moral judgments. Our moral sense seems to be sufficiently sophisticated to handle discriminations between moral and nonmoral judgments if we are careful. If we exclude factors that are outside of the agent's range of control, then we are narrowing the scope of our evaluations, but we are also maintaining a consistent distinction between moral and nonmoral judgments.[54] Once we exclude factors outside an agent's control, we assess the morality of an agent's actions only on the basis of the choices made that were in the control of the agent to make. On these terms, luck in circumstances is clearly not moral.[55] That the pressures different agents face can vary substantially only points to the unfairness of life. To this, Kant's response would be that nothing about the moral sphere guarantees that worldly happiness will accompany morally correct choices. That is why he says that gifts of fortune relate to happiness but do not violate the morally good will. What Nagel is asking us to accept, however, is that the circumstance is responsible for the morality of our choice. Is the circumstance an aspect or occasion of the decision, or is it a cause? For Kant, it is an aspect, while for Nagel it is a cause. Kant can see it as an aspect because in his view freedom is transcendental and not subject to the mechanistic determinism of the phenomenal realm. Nagel, for his part, has no theoretical place for genuine human freedom and so sees the question from inside the framework of mechanistic determinism. Hence, the circumstance is the cause and the luck for him is moral.

What this category also calls into question is the Kantian conception of the good will as the great equalizer. The logic is that if the good will is something that is invulnerable to chance, then everyone has an equal chance to be morally good.[56] What Nagel's example really shows is that the moral sphere is not necessarily a sphere that makes people's lives equal. One does not have to conclude from this, however, that luck in circumstances is moral luck so long as one does not accept that there can be genuine moral dilemmas, situations in which one cannot help but commit a moral evil.[57] Arguing for the existence or nonexistence of such dilemmas is beyond the scope of this book, but since the existence of moral dilemmas is considered an open matter among ethicists, it is clear that not all ethicists would automatically agree that circumstantial luck is moral.[58] Thus, Nagel's example, powerful though it may be, can lead us to conclude that life is indeed unfair, without also concluding that it is morally unfair.

While Nagel's two categories of Kantian gifts of fortune do not directly constitute moral luck as Nagel claims, they do show that luck deeply affects the lives we lead. How our actions turn out, and the very situations in which we must act, are not entirely within our control. Although Nagel's categories are not instances of moral luck (when the moral is understood to involve agent control and not merely legal and social conventions), they are nonetheless two ways in which luck profoundly affects us. Moreover, even though these two categories are not direct evidence of moral luck, they may qualify as "indirect" instances of moral luck insofar as they bear on a person's character development. This brings us to Nagel's other two categories, which relate to character.

"Character"

Constitutive luck and luck in the way one is determined by antecedent circumstances (antecedent luck) make stronger challenges to the claim of invulnerability in the moral sphere. To the extent that they determine/influence a person's character development, they affect the very ability of a person to act well because a person's character, good or bad, qualifies her or his ability and proclivity to act in life. If a person is either born with personality features such as temperament that make the development of a morally good character difficult or has experiences in life that shatter the ability to act well, then that person can be considered to have had the deck stacked against her.

Constitutive luck. Regarding constitutive luck, Nagel's point is that some people simply have inborn personal characteristics that are more challenging from a moral point of view. Since they are still asked to function morally, it appears to be a case of moral bad luck. But is it? Again, if a necessary feature of morality is agent control, then innate personality factors outside of one's control would not be directly subject to moral evaluation.[59] Moreover, the agent would not be morally condemned for acts that were directly caused by these features if they truly were beyond the control of the agent. The actions may have legal consequences, and they may result in negative social judgments, but these judgments are not of what is truly moral, and to take them as such is to move too freely between different types of assessments.

Luck in antecedent circumstances. Luck in antecedent circumstances is the most compelling of Nagel's categories as a genuine kind of moral luck. Here, we are asked to consider not just how someone acts in one particularly difficult situation, but how the course of a person's entire life can be affected by something that happened to that person that was all or largely outside of that person's control. Claudia Card has called attention to this type of luck in a particularly powerful way in *Unnatural Lottery*, in which she asks us to consider antecedent circumstances such as child abuse as matters of luck with relevance in the moral sphere.[60] It is difficult to imagine child abuse not having a significant impact on an individual's character development. But is the experience of child abuse a case of bad luck that is also bad moral luck?

Antecedent luck is not confined to cases in which the antecedent circumstance was something that happened to a person. Even prior choices in which a person did have control can significantly impair a person as she lives and grows. This is where luck in consequences and luck in circumstances reenter as possible contributors to moral luck. Recall Nagel's example of the successful and unsuccessful rescue attempts. A person may make a just and careful decision to attempt to rescue an individual when no other possibility of saving the person presents itself. Suppose, however, that the attempt fails, that the rescuer inadvertently and even unavoidably drops the person to her death. At that very moment, another, more promising rescuer appears. Surely the failed rescuer will live with self-reproach forever and quite possibly this self-reproach will affect this person's ability to act well in a variety of situations. Courage, for example, may be forever beyond the reach of this person, even in situations in which a lack of courage seems immoral. Is this luck in antecedent circumstances a case of moral luck? Certainly, luck in antecedent circumstances can have the appearance of moral luck. Things can happen to people that appear to change their ability to act morally. Experiences of victimization, such as child abuse, or tragic failures, such as in failed rescue attempts, are good candidates as factors that can compromise a person morally.

As in the case of constitutive luck, however, if one continues to answer the question based upon a traditional understanding of morality as involving agent control, then a sufficiently reflective analysis will take the antecedent circumstances as factors that limit agent control and so place their effects outside the moral sphere. This will not necessarily shrink the moral sphere to the vanishing point as Nagel suggests, however. There may be extreme cases in which all ability to make meaningful choices is destroyed by antecedent circumstances, but these are more properly described as tragedies than as cases of moral luck as Nagel presents it. More often, however, a less radical constriction in a person's ability to function morally may occur. And with only some constriction there is still room for choice, control, and eventual growth. A person may never be the same after a particular experience, but the person may still continue to develop and make meaningful choices. Even character is not fixed, however developed it may be. Future choices may always bear the markings of a past event without being completely determined by them.[61] Luck is involved, but not moral luck, at least not in the sense Nagel uses it.

Critical Assessment

The chief difficulty with Nagel's essay is that he attempts to hang on to a notion of human responsibility that requires an acknowledgment of free choice, yet since he does not account for free choice theoretically he is left with saying merely that we must continue to act as if we were morally responsible and free because that understanding is central to what we think it means to be human. This is a good faith move on his part, but one he undertakes because he is operating with a view of the world that offers him no real theoretical room for an account of freedom. In Nagel's essay, then, we have the curious case of a philosopher rejecting Kant's claim of the invulnerability of the good will because the philosopher, Nagel, fails to reject the scientific paradigm that Kant himself accepts for the phenomenal world. The difference, of course, is that Nagel accepts only part of Kant's worldview, rejecting as he does Kant's metaphysical solution to the problem that the Newtonian worldview creates for freedom. However, Nagel's "as if" move, so roundly critiqued by Rorty, is unnecessary if we accept the implications of the new scientific paradigm for a theoretical grounding of human freedom. It must be acknowledged, of course, that the work in chapter 2 creates only a plausible theoretical grounding for freedom, not a proof that it exists. So to an extent, one must always choose one's position on the existence of genuine human freedom. However, with the grounding provided by contemporary scientific theory, one is no longer simply choosing to go with experience over theory; instead, one is choosing to go with experience made plausible by theory. And if we allow freedom back into the picture, then moral evaluation, human responsibility, and the possibility of character development despite all kinds of bad luck are back in the picture, though, as I will soon suggest, they may need to take a different place in the picture.

It is not enough, however, to see where Nagel fails to critique fully the assumptions underlying Kant's view. Were we to do only that, we would miss the clarity with which Nagel demonstrates our profound vulnerability to luck, to factors outside our control, as well as our vulnerability to freedom, to factors under our control and others' control that affect us and generate future possibilities for us.

Just as it is not possible to prove the existence of human freedom decisively, it is also not possible to specify with exactitude how vulnerable we are to the conditions of existence, even to human freedom. We must be satisfied with something more modest—the recognition that we are vulnerable, indeed deeply vulnerable, to the conditions of our existence, but that to the degree that we are also free, we are not totally vulnerable. And since we cannot, in the final analysis, say definitively just how vulnerable we are, another facet of the moral luck debate as shaped by Nagel is called into question, and that is the idea that the main point of examining moral luck is to determine whether or not it makes sense to hold humans morally responsible for their actions. The simple answer is that we can be morally responsible to the degree that we have freedom. But if morality is indeed linked to freedom, then we must ask, Is the evaluation of moral responsibility the point of freedom? If we are unable in theory to specify our degree of vulnerability beyond acknowledging that it is deep, does it make sense to pursue the determination of moral responsibility as the central point of ethical inquiry? Or are this and related ethical endeavors more properly described as important but not primary ethical tasks?

Acceptance: An Alternative Approach

As noted above, an important feature of Nagel's article is that in his careful description of the four categories of luck he illustrates how extreme and uneven luck is in life. At various times we all seem to have some good luck and some bad luck, of each of the types covered by Nagel. This observation is directly in line with the description of existence as deeply dependent given in the first chapter of this book. Nagel's essay drives home the further realization that this luck does not just even out in the end for each of us. Some people have such bad antecedent luck that their lives are in a real sense ruined. Children are born every day into such desperate and abusive situations that their bodies and minds are forever damaged. Others live lives graced with luck in the natural lottery[62] as well as in the main circumstances and outcomes of their lives. No appeal to the invulnerability of the good will can convince us that there is a basic, underlying fairness to life.

How, then, can we look at morality in a way that provides meaningful insight to our existence in the face of our deep vulnerability to the conditions of life, conditions that often strike us with their manifest unfairness? If we agree that the new scientific worldview offers validation for the abiding human experience of freedom, then we can answer that in the face of life's unfairness, in the face of our vulnerability to the conditions of our existence, to what happens to us as well as to features of our own personal makeup, we are still free. We can even be so vulnerable to luck in its various forms that our ability to act well is compromised (so that we are not even morally responsible at times). We are moreover deeply limited beings. There are serious and real limits to what we can do and accomplish, to how long we can live and how well we can live. In even these circumstances, however, there remains something that we can do with our freedom. We can accept. We can accept ourselves, our lives, including the events and processes that contributed to our becoming who we are; we can accept the people in our lives and even the very conditions of our existence.[63] Acceptance replaces assignment of moral responsibility as the primary ethical task.

Looking at the fundamental moral task of freedom as acceptance helps us understand our invulnerability and live with our vulnerability by giving us a new way of seeing morality.[64] Moral evaluation of actions and agents takes place under a new light because now the evaluation is conducted in order to facilitate acceptance. But a word of caution is in order here. The acceptance I am referring to is an acceptance of our own true selves and of others in the context of our existence. It is not an easy acceptance. It involves discovering and developing ourselves, and helping others to do the same, so that what is accepted is what we truly are, not whatever we happen to be doing or trying to do. Moreover, it is an active, efficacious acceptance that opposes mere resignation. It also involves moral evaluation, but now the point of the moral evaluation is not judgment but acceptance. Judgment as moral discernment aids discovery and discovery of what is genuine must precede acceptance.

Fleshing out just how acceptance can function as a moral task, and in particular how we can understand our obligations toward ourselves and others in terms of acceptance, requires a full chapter. The fruitfulness of this new approach is thus articulated in chapter 5. At this point, it is possible only to sketch how acceptance can function as a moral task.

So far in this chapter, the analysis of the moral luck debate in the light of the new scientific paradigm, with its theoretical grounding for freedom, has yielded support for the view of the human person as not completely vulnerable to the conditions of existence. Nothing has been found, because of our capacity for freedom, to discredit fully the Kantian view that we possess a degree of invulnerability to luck, to what is beyond our control, although the grounding for freedom is substantially different than Kant's postulate of transcendental freedom. And the capacity for freedom, as Nagel so correctly intuits, is fundamental to our self-understanding. Each person possesses some degree of invulnerability to the conditions of existence and each person is a being of value, capable of acting in freedom. As will be suggested in chapter 5, this freedom has as its ultimate purpose acceptance of God, but this fundamental task can only be accomplished through an acceptance of one's enduring identity, one's true self, in the context of all of the ways in which each of us experiences vulnerability. Obviously, underlying this new approach to ethics is a view of the human person that is at odds with Rorty's in that it takes for granted the notions that we have a 'self' and that some things that are important for ethics can indeed be discovered. But since it is based on an understanding of human persons as particular beings whose individuality arises from unique ways of experiencing fundamental conditions of existence, it does not assume an essentialized notion of the self beyond what the conditions of existence can account for: particularity, freedom, and value. In this sense, it assumes an anthropology that is close to Rahner's, but without requiring his metaphysical assumptions.

Before we can go further in considering what acceptance entails, we need to understand more about this task in the face of vulnerability. Nagel's analysis of his four candidates for kinds of moral luck has helped us gain a deeper appreciation of the myriad ways in which we are vulnerable to both factors beyond our control and the consequences of our own decisions. Although it is not possible to go beyond this and specify just how deep our vulnerability is, other than to say that it is not total, we are still left asking what this can mean for us. We begin to answer that question when we recognize that our fundamental moral task is accepting our true selves, which involves accepting ourselves as deeply contingent and finite beings. This leads us to part II of this book, "Implications for Ethics." For a concrete presentation of the invulnerability of identity and the importance of acceptance in the face of deep vulnerability, an ethical analysis of Charles Dickens's treatment of vulnerability and acceptance in *Our Mutual Friend* is the subject of the next chapter. Then chapter 5 offers a much fuller description of how acceptance can help us understand our obligations to ourselves and one another in the context of our deep and mutual dependencies and limitations.

Notes

1. According to Richard Rorty, it is precisely with Plato that Western philosophy took the wrong turn from which it has never recovered. See *Objectivity, Relativism, and Truth* (New York: Cambridge University Press, 1991), 32, 71.

2. On the invulnerability of Boethian virtue, see Timothy Jackson, "The Disconsolation of Theology," *Journal of Religious Ethics* 20, no. 1 (Spring 1992), 2.

3. As Bernard Williams puts it, the whole point of morality and rational agency is to escape contingency. See his postscript to *Moral Luck*, ed. Daniel Statman (Albany: State University of New York Press, 1993), 251, 257.

4. John Calvin describes the comfort of Providence in *Institutes of the Christian Religion*, 2 vols., ed. John T. McNeill, trans. Ford Lewis Battles, Library of Christian Classics, vol. 21 (Philadelphia: Westminster, 1960), I.16.3. Calvin also says, "What then? Does nothing happen by chance, nothing by contingency? I reply: Basil the Great has truly said that 'fortune' and 'chance' are pagan terms, with whose significance the minds of the godly ought not to be occupied. For if every success is God's blessing, and calamity and adversity his curse, *no place now remains in human affairs for fortune or chance*" (I.16.8.; italics mine).

5. Calvin, *Institutes*, III.21.1.

6. Martha C. Nussbaum, *The Fragility of Goodness: Luck and Ethics in Greek Tragedy and Philosophy* (New York: Cambridge University Press, 1986), 18.

7. See Anthony Kenny, "Aristotle on Moral Luck," in *Modern Thinkers and Ancient Thinkers*, ed. Robert W. Sharples (London: University College London Press, 1993), 161–62.

8. Williams, *Moral Luck*, postscript, 251.

9. Temptations to read luck as synonymous with contingency must be resisted, though even the literature is misleading on this score. Luck is used to indicate that which is beyond our control. In that respect, it encompasses less than contingency. Sometimes, what we are dependent (contingent) upon is or has been under our control. Only the specific form of luck in consequences captures this dependency, but it is not generally included in ideas of luck.

10. Although Plato's quest for pure form provides an invulnerability to the conditions of existence, not just a moral invulnerability, he does have a specific understanding of moral invulnerability that results from loving the good. As Charles Taylor puts it, on Plato's view, those who love the good "cannot help but be morally good." Taylor, *Sources of the Self: The Making of the Modern Identity* (Cambridge: Harvard University Press, 1989), 122–23.

11. Thomas Nagel, "Moral Luck," in *Mortal Questions* (New York: Cambridge University Press, 1979), 36.

12. Recall from chapter 2 that Rorty considers the exercise pedagogical because, although we *could* make such predictions, we would only do so occasionally, and not as a part of daily life.

13. Nagel makes an interesting point about predictability and freedom when he says that predictability does not pose a problem for freedom and argues that one can choose predictably. See Nagel, "Subjective and Objective," *Mortal Questions*, 198. He has a point in the case of short-term predictability. However, Rorty argues that we can predict far into the future and do so *reliably*. Such confidence in the correctness of one's predictions challenges the possibility of any genuine freedom.

14. Rorty does simply set aside the freedom/mechanism debate, saying that it is an "artificial opposition" that is part of a language game that no longer serves us. See Rorty, "Non-reductive Physicalism," *Objectivity, Relativism, and Truth*, 125.

15. Rorty, *Consequences of Pragmatism* (Minneapolis: University of Minnesota Press, 1982), xxxiii–xxxiv.

16. Nagel, "Moral Luck," 24–38.

17. Nagel, "Moral Luck," 35.

18. Rorty, *Consequences of Pragmatism*, xxxvi–xxxvii. By intuitive realism Rorty means that Nagel remains committed to a notion of philosophical truth to which various accounts "are trying to be 'adequate.'"

19. Rorty, *Consequences of Pragmatism*, xxxvi. In this passage, Rorty says that Nagel's move is no better or worse than the pragmatist's dismissal of the subject altogether. In his later works, however, he clearly presents a view of the human person that says that an active self is mistaken. See chapter 2 of this book.

20. On this, see Nagel, "What Is It Like to Be a Bat?," *Mortal Questions*, 165–80.

21. Immanuel Kant, *Foundations of the Metaphysic of Morals*, first section, third paragraph; quoted in Nagel, "Moral Luck," 24.

22. Immanuel Kant, "On a Supposed Right to Lie from Altruistic Motives," in *Moral Absolutism*, ed. Joram Graf Haber (Lanham, Md.: Rowman & Littlefield, 1994), 15–19. See page 17 regarding consequences. Kant also argues in *Groundwork* that prudence is not an argument in favor of lying because "to foresee the consequences is not so easy that I can be sure there is no chance . . . of this [lie] proving far more disadvantageous than all the ills I now think to avoid. . . ." *Groundwork of the Metaphysic of Morals*, trans. H. J. Paton (New York: Harper and Row, 1964), 70.

23. The moral luck literature is uniform on this point. "Luck" is used to designate what is outside of the agent's control, with no restrictions as to randomness or noncausality.

24. Nagel, "Moral Luck," 25.

25. Williams, postscript to *Moral Luck*, 251.

26. Williams, "Moral Luck," *Moral Luck: Philosophical Papers 1973–1980* (New York: Cambridge University Press, 1981), 20–39. For helpful discussions of the differences between Williams and Nagel, see Daniel Statman's introduction to *Moral Luck*, ed. Statman, 1–15, and Judith Andre's "Nagel, Williams, and Moral Luck," also in *Moral Luck*, ed. Statman, 123–29.

27. Nagel, "Moral Luck," 27.

28. Paul Ricoeur offers an excellent example of the way that paradox functions in *Freedom and Nature*. There he states, "Assurance of resolution is always the covert reason for paradox: in a certain way we are always confident of the unity of what we break up as we conceive of it." There is a point of unity between the apparently contradictory sides of a paradox, and so as we explore the apparent contradiction we can still know that unity rather than fragmentation will be the endpoint of the exploration. Ricoeur, *Freedom and Nature: The Voluntary and the Involuntary*, trans. Erazim V. Kohák (Evanston, Ill.: Northwestern University Press, 1966), 353.

29. Nagel, "Moral Luck," 37–38. Nagel's essay, "Subjective and Objective," *Mortal Questions*, 196–213, is explicitly devoted to this topic. He also covers it in detail in "Freedom," in *The View from Nowhere* (New York: Oxford University Press, 1986), 110–37. It is interesting to note how deeply Kantian Nagel's entire approach is. Compare his idea of the paradox resulting from two perspectives with Kant's "two standpoints" in Kant's *Groundwork*, 124. Of course, Nagel does not involve Kantian metaphysics in his two perspectives.

30. Nagel, "Moral Luck," 28. For simplicity, they will be referred to as constitutive luck, luck in circumstances, antecedent luck, and luck in consequences.

31. Kant, *Groundwork*, 61.

32. Nagel, "Moral Luck," 25.

33. Nagel, "Moral Luck," 25.

34. Contributors to the debate do question at times whether or not a particular judgment is moral. For example, see Judith Jarvis Thomson's "Morality and Bad Luck," in *Moral Luck*, ed. Statman, 195–215, especially 204–5, regarding luck in consequences. However, the basic question of what is meant by 'moral' is not addressed.

35. Such a distinction parallels the distinction between nonmoral (or ontic) and moral evil. In the first order, one is morally responsible for moral evil. It could then be argued that one is morally obligated to attend to the nonmorally evil consequences of one's actions without actually failing to distinguish between the two types of responsibility, as Nagel does. For discussions of the distinction between moral and nonmoral evil, see Peter Knauer, "The Hermeneutic Function of the Principle of Double Effect," and Louis Janssens, "Ontic and Moral Evil," pages 1–39 and 40–93, respectively, in *Readings in Moral Theology No. 1: Moral Norms and Catholic Tradition*, ed. Charles E. Curran and Richard A. McCormick (New York: Paulist, 1979).

36. Nagel, "Moral Luck," 25, 29.

37. Nagel, "Moral Luck," 25.

38. Thomson offers an interesting analysis in terms of different senses of blame, not all of which are moral, in "Morality and Bad Luck." Judith Andre also discusses issues of praise and blame as distinct from Kantian moral judgments, but does so in support of her argument for an Aristotelian rather than Kantian moral evaluation. Andre, "Nagel, Williams, and Moral Luck," in *Moral Luck*, ed. Statman.

39. Kant, *Groundwork*, 65.

40. Kant, *Groundwork*, 75.

41. Objections that one driver retains better driving capabilities when intoxicated and so is less likely to hit a pedestrian are therefore ruled out by Nagel's example. See Andre, "Nagel, Williams, and Moral Luck," 127. Norvin Richards, in "Luck and Desert" (in *Moral Luck*, ed. Statman, 171), suggests a parallel point for the reckless driver who is sufficiently alert and skillful to drive at high speeds. However, Nagel may be able to rule out such objections only to his hypothetical case. One will never know if both drivers would have hit the pedestrian or if one would still have had the resources with which to swerve to avoid hitting the pedestrian. We lead particular

lives, not hypothetical ones, and can properly make moral evaluations only of what we actually do, or what we will to do.

42. This is what Nicholas Rescher says in "Moral Luck," in *Moral Luck*, ed. Statman, 141–66. In Rescher's words, "People who drive their cars home from an office party in a thoroughly intoxicated condition, indifferent to the danger to themselves and heedless of the risks they are creating for others, are equally guilty in the eyes of *morality* (as opposed to *legality*) whether they kill someone along the way or not" (158). This is only one possibility. It is also possible to claim that there is a morally significant difference without appealing to differences in punishment. See note 41.

43. Joel Feinberg, "Equal Punishment for Failed Attempts: Some Bad but Instructive Arguments Against It," *Arizona Law Review* 37 (1995): 117–33. Quotations from pages 119 and 118, respectively.

44. Intention has an inner dimension to it, but as Oliver O'Donovan points out, "The intention of an act is implied in the structure of the act, and not in some moment of psychological clarity in the actor." See "Intention," *Peace and Certainty* (Grand Rapids, Mich.: Eerdmans, 1989), 78.

45. Of course, showing that the agent had a motive is part of a case against the agent, but it is not proof of a crime. The difference between intention and motive parallels that between object and end, in Thomas Aquinas's terms in *Summa Theologica* (Westminster, Md.: Christian Classics, 1948), I–II, 18. It is far easier to determine if one has pulled the trigger of a gun than why one has pulled the trigger.

46. Jeremy Bentham also recognized the difference between intention and motive, giving greater particular significance to intention in the evaluation of an act. Of note is that Bentham's stated purpose in evaluating an act is to determine punishment for the good of society. See *Principles of Morals and Legislation* (London: Clarendon Press, 1907), 70–71. Motives, which give rise to intentions, are all ultimately either pain or pleasure, according to Bentham (97–103).

47. Compensation is conceptually close to retribution, but usually involves monetary repayment.

48. Georg W. F. Hegel, *Hegel's Philosophy of Right*, trans. T. M. Knox (New York: Oxford University Press, 1967), 71–73, 141, and 247, n. 64.

49. Bentham opens his chapter on punishments and offenses by declaring, "We have seen that the general object of all laws is to prevent mischief." Bentham, *Principles of Morals and Legislation*, 178.

50. Nagel also appeals to our emotional reaction to the different outcomes, as well as to our own self-evaluations.

51. Nagel, "Moral Luck," 33–34.

52. Nagel, "Moral Luck," 34.

53. Nagel, "Moral Luck," 25.

54. Nagel objects to this narrowing of scope, noting especially that it involves isolating the will. However, he makes no argument for including these other factors in moral evaluations, resting his case solely on the argument that in practice we seem to include them. See Nagel, "Moral Luck," 31–32.

55. Two contributors to the moral luck debate make interesting points in this regard. Rescher observes of morally similar agents facing different circumstances, "Their moral *record* may differ, but their moral *standing* does not." Rescher, "Moral Luck," 154. Richards also defers to the consistency of character when he says that we will "enact our character," whatever the circumstances. Richards, "Luck and Desert," 174–75.

56. Kenny refers to this as "the ideal of equality of opportunity" in "Aristotle on Moral Luck," 167. Kenny's point is that this egalitarian push is part of the problem with Kantian morality, as opposed to an Aristotelian morality, which tries to "mak[e] the best of the unfair world we live in" (170).

57. Nagel refers to such a possibility in "Moral Luck," *Mortal Questions*, 34, n. 9. For a refutation of this possibility, see Timothy Jackson's four arguments against the existence of dilemmas in "Disconsolation of Theology," 16–17.

58. Indeed, ethicists who reject it outright as moral luck are Kenny ("Aristotle on Moral Luck," 160) and Michael Zimmerman ("Luck and Moral Responsibility," in *Moral Luck*, ed. Statman, 230), as well as Rescher and Richards as cited in note 55, above.

59. There is also the argument that we all have to develop morally and shape our personal characteristics. Virtue theory tells us that it is possible to shape our inborn capacities. Part of being morally responsible selves is taking responsibility for the selves that we are and have grown into, given our choices as we have grown. Nagel's position does not rule this out. His contention might be restated as this: it is easier for some people to grow in virtue than it is for others.

60. Claudia Card, *The Unnatural Lottery: Character and Moral Luck* (Philadelphia: Temple University Press, 1996). Among Card's other examples in this excellent work are domestic abuse, sexual assault, and erotic orientation.

61. Card thus emphasizes the future orientation of responsibility and chides both Nagel and Williams for emphasizing backward-looking responsibility. Card, *Unnatural Lottery*, 23.

62. Natural lottery is the term associated with John Rawls's description of the distribution of "natural assets—that is, natural talents and abilities." See Rawls, *A Theory of Justice* (Cambridge, Mass.: Belknap, 1971), 72.

63. This acceptance is a genuine choice, for we can accept or reject ourselves. Paul Ricoeur also notes this basic task of freedom when he says, "Freedom is the possibility of not accepting myself." Ricoeur, *Freedom and Nature*, 445.

64. Acceptance is the fundamental moral task of freedom because it is freedom's primary task (in line with our primary religious task of acceptance) and because it grounds other moral uses of freedom. The religious dimension of this fundamental task is explored in chapter 5.

PART TWO

Implications for Ethics

CHAPTER FOUR

Vulnerability and Acceptance in *Our Mutual Friend*: A Case Study

If the consideration of moral luck in chapter 3 yielded the view that we are deeply but not wholly vulnerable to factors beyond our control, it also brought to the fore how far-reaching the vulnerability we do possess is. The particular lives that we lead and our ability to act well are both influenced by factors we do not control. Contingency and finitude as fundamental conditions of our existence are felt in each aspect of our lives. In chapter 1, the primary explicators chosen for contingency and finitude were dependency and limitation, respectively. To say that we are contingent is to say that who we are and how we live are deeply dependent on a multiplicity of factors. At the same time we are also finite, experiencing our finitude as limitation of being, identity, capacity, and even possibility. Each one of us is the particular person that she is and only that person. We each can have only a part of being, of life. What we are able to do and when we are able to do it are also subject to limitation.

However, this vulnerability to the conditions of our existence is not total. Human beings are more than the sum total of the stories that they can tell about their lives, more than a tallying of their actions and environment, as the pragmatist view would have it. The consideration of moral luck in chapter 3 turned aside the view that the deep dependency and limitation of existence extend to the moral realm by necessitating us to be or act immorally, once the parameters of what can be considered moral are properly seen and accounted for. When factors are completely beyond a person's control, for example, then that person cannot be held morally accountable for actions that result directly from these factors. But when a person is truly an agent, with some area for free choice relative to an action entailing a positive or negative obligation, then that person's action can be properly subject to moral evaluation. The consideration of moral luck in chapter 3 thus affirmed that we are not wholly determined by what we depend on; we are more than what we do and what happens to us. There is something to each person that is uniquely valuable, uniquely enduring. Because we are also free, we are deeply vulnerable to the conditions of our existence, but not utterly so. And this freedom helps us act out of an enduring aspect of our selves, who we deeply and truly are. Thus, at our deepest level, we are free even as we are vulnerable, and it is in our exercise of freedom that we act as moral beings.

At the conclusion of chapter 3, the question was asked, what is this freedom *for?* The answer offered was acceptance: of our selves, our lives, the people in our lives, and ultimately even of the conditions of existence. This is the fundamental moral task, for it is only when we fully accept ourselves as unique and yet vulnerable beings that we are able to fully realize ourselves as responsible actors. And it is only as responsible actors that we are able to act creatively in the world as we grow and develop as human beings. However, what this acceptance entails and how important it is to the very possibility of our leading truly moral lives is not self-evident. To obtain a clearer understanding of this task of acceptance, an examination of a concrete portrayal of it is in order. Charles Dickens's *Our Mutual Friend* offers a particularly useful opportunity in this regard, for it provides a sustained dramatization of the need for this fundamental acceptance of self and is offered with a full recognition of the deep vulnerability of existence. Dickens poses the issue as one of identity and, in his intricate thematic style, engages the issue in a multiplicity of ways to show us not only the importance of self-acceptance but also the various ways in which we avoid this task and the harms that result to ourselves and those around us as a consequence of this avoidance.

Dickens's *Our Mutual Friend* is also a fitting resource because in this novel Dickens exhibits in narrative form a view of the self not unlike the one argued for in the theological anthropology of Karl Rahner.[1] Throughout his career, Dickens wrestled with the question of the effects of social evils, especially poverty, on individuals. In the context of this exploration, Dickens showed a keen sympathy for the vulnerability of individuals to their social situation. However, he clearly resisted any idea of complete vulnerability.[2] His novels show people sometimes bearing even severe marks of social evil and yet maintaining their integrity and dignity.[3] As A. E. Dyson notes, "The moral differences between people coming from the same unpropitious background: this theme fascinated Dickens all his life."[4] Correspondingly, wealth and social privilege do not confer moral goodness upon individuals in Dickens's novels.[5] Dickens does not explicitly argue for his view of human freedom, but he clearly gives us a picture of human beings as possessing some degree of freedom, and therefore some degree of invulnerability in the moral sphere. A Rortian view of the human person as utterly contingent appears to be completely out of place in Dickens's novels. To use Dyson's words again, Dickens "was certainly not a mechanical determinist."[6]

By the time that Charles Dickens turned to writing *Our Mutual Friend*, the last novel that he was to complete, he had already explored finitude/limitation as a condition of existence. In an earlier novel, *Little Dorrit*, Dickens examined the way in which we experience limitation and even need to create it for ourselves. Indeed, in *Little Dorrit* Dickens gives life to the words Otto Rank later used: "*we . . . create* out of our freedom, a prison."[7] In *Little Dorrit* Dickens is also concerned to depict how we handle our finitude, but he does so with a kind of resignation. The most that we can hope for in the existentially weary world of this novel is redemption, but not transformation. Amy Dorrit, the novel's heroine, copes with finitude and is able to be a savior to other characters in the novel, but none of them, including Amy Dorrit, are truly able to transcend the prisons of their existence. *Little Dorrit* thus provides a detailed description of how we cope with our finitude in ways that perpetuate our limitation, but offers little hope for any kind of individually initiated transformation that allows for a transcendence of this condition of existence. The only hope that *Little Dorrit* offers is of meeting another human being who can function as the kind of worldly savior that Amy Dorrit is to her father and Arthur Clennam, giving us some degree of dignity and purpose in our constricted lives.

Fortunately, the dark vision of life presented in *Little Dorrit* is not Dickens's last word. In the novels written between *Little Dorrit* and *Our Mutual Friend*, Dickens explores more creatively, and moves toward, an idea of personal identity and self-acceptance. The first of these novels, *A Tale of Two Cities*, is thematically closer to *Little Dorrit*, and the second, *Great Expectations*, is closer to *Our Mutual Friend*. In *A Tale of Two Cities*, the very possibility of hope for a meaningful life is created only by Sidney Carton's decision to die in Charles Darnay's place. Thus Carton functions like Amy Dorrit, as a savior. Here, however, the novel closes more hopefully, with self-giving love creating a genuine possibility for happiness for Charles Darnay and his family to be and freeing Sidney Carton to experience complete peace. A significantly greater move is made in *Great Expectations*, for here the focus is redemption, not by another but by oneself in one's own act of self-definition, an act that involves a relinquishing of idealizations about oneself and others to make a genuine acceptance of self and others possible. By the time that Dickens commenced writing *Our Mutual Friend*, then, he was able to give us the fruit of the explorations of these ideas in the earlier novels. *Our Mutual Friend* has not the darkness of *Little Dorrit*, the drama of *A Tale of Two Cities*, or the emotion of *Great Expectations*. What it has instead is great balance, vision, and complexity in its treatment of human existence as a moral task.

Our Mutual Friend offers, then, a literary approach to the same questions that have been pursued in the previous chapters. With it, it is possible to continue and expand our examination of how we live given the conditions of our existence: finitude and contingency. In this novel, the primary task is a self-acceptance that sometimes means transformation and change,[8] but always involves the embracing of one's true identity. J. Hillis Miller speaks directly to the heart of the novel when he observes that in it "no one can escape his given place."[9] This is not a comment upon social structure, but upon existence. Who we are, our very identity, is realized only in and through our particular location. In the world of *Our Mutual Friend*, human existence is recognized as situated existence. Our identity is thus deeply contingent. Yet, as portrayed here, context does not wholly determine who we are. It remains for us to understand our situatedness and then actively to accept it as we accept ourself and claim our identity. Once we do this, we transcend the givenness of our situated existence and make it the springboard of our actions. Although we will never change our original place in the world (in the sense that it will always be what it was) and we will not be so transformed that all of the scars of our lives will be healed, we will be able to use our freedom creatively as we grow and develop ourselves, no longer completely held back by what has happened to us in our lives. The key to understanding this perspective in the novel is to see that Dickens's portrayals of important features of our particular existence are themselves neutral.[10] We are situated but not fated, for the meaning and value of our lives is finally determined by the ways in which we accept or reject them, the ways in which we become ourselves in relation to the givenness of our lives.

The secondary literature addressing this novel has devoted considerable space to the question of the value given to the major symbols in the novel.[11] Dickens often used one primary symbol in his novels, the fog of *Bleak House* being the best example. Clearly, in that novel fog symbolizes the blinding effect of England's judicial system in particular and its public policy in general. There is no question that the fog has a negative value. In *Our Mutual Friend*, two symbols, the river and the dust mounds, are central. Unlike the fog in *Bleak House*, however, these two symbols are ambiguous. John Lucas has even suggested that they are not symbols at all because they do not have a univocal value.[12] This very confusion is a matter of design, however, for it reveals

Dickens's point: that is, one cannot look at the dust mounds of the novel, see merely waste and refuse, and decide that they have a negative worth, or that they immediately reveal the decay of society.[13] Instead, one is forced to see that dust mounds are dust mounds; how one relates to them determines whether they have a positive or negative value in one's own task of self-acceptance and the further task of accepting others. These two major symbols, the dust mounds and the river, symbolize the need to see not an arbitrarily assigned or fated value in the concrete aspects of existence, but a possibility for moral action.

Dickens opens *Our Mutual Friend* with a scene in which the true ambiguity of the value of the river is introduced. We are immediately presented with the appearance of a "boat of a dirty and disreputable appearance, with two figures in it."[14] The girl, we are told, looks enough like the man to be recognized as his daughter. Beyond that, we are only given indications that whatever his occupation on the river might be, it is not an honorable one. In the paragraphs that ensue, we learn that the daughter (Lizzie Hexam) is ashamed of the work and seeks to hide her face as if to hide from the reality. Her father remonstrates:

> "It's my belief that you hate the sight of the very river."
> "I—I do not like it, father."
> "As if it wasn't your living! As if it wasn't meat and drink to you!"
> At these latter words the girl shivered again, and for a moment paused in her rowing, seeming to turn deadly faint. It escaped his attention, for he was glancing over the stern at something the boat had in tow.
> "How can you be so thankless to your best friend, Lizzie? The very fire that warmed you when you were a baby, was picked out of the river alongside the coal barges. The very basket that you slept in, the tide washed ashore. The very rockers that I put it upon to make a cradle of it, I cut out of a piece of wood that drifted from some ship or another." (I, 1)

The river may have negative associations for her, but it has also been the source of goods used in her nurture, and thus not wholly bad for her. By the close of the chapter we have enough clues to surmise that the occupation of the man is to relieve the river's corpses of their possessions. His daughter finds this a dreadful enterprise, hence her negative view of the river, and yet we are also given to see that the man does not engage in it dreadfully. His assessment of the morality of his action may be mistaken, but he undertakes his occupation as a justifiable one. By presenting us with both views from the start, Dickens indicates that Lizzie's view is not to be taken as *the* view. Although the full complexity of Dickens's treatment of the river is not evident until some fifty-four chapters later, even in this first chapter it is clear that Dickens wishes to guard against his readers making a simplistic assessment of the opening scene.[15]

The Plot

Our Mutual Friend is a long and complicated novel, with as complex a plot as ever a Dickens novel had.[16] To do justice to this complexity, a fairly long summary of the plot is required. The novel actually has two plot lines, the Boffin plot and the Lizzie-Eugene plot, which are interconnected at various points but with a major link in our mutual friend, John Harmon.[17] Since the focus of the ethical analysis of the novel is on characters from the Lizzie-Eugene plot, more detail is provided for that plot line. But first, some key points from the Boffin plot line need to be given.

The Boffin Plot Line

Early in the novel we learn that a corpse has been found by none other than Gaffer Hexam, Lizzie's father, and that the identification papers on the corpse belong to John Harmon. Harmon, we are told, has been en route by sea from "Somewhere"[18] to collect the vast inheritance that his mean-spirited father had amassed through his dust mounds. In order for John to collect, however, he must satisfy one significant term of the will: he must marry Bella Wilfer, a pretty and spirited young woman whom the elder Harmon had seen when she was a child. The younger Harmon had left his father years earlier, and was filled with mistrust toward him. During the trip to England, he devised a plan whereby a man of similar build would take his place, while he himself would slip out of sight for a few days so that he could observe Miss Bella Wilfer and determine whether or not he should marry her. John falls victim to his own scheme, however, when an attempt is made to murder him and assume his identity. John escapes but his double is murdered. Deciding to stay "dead" for a time, John assumes first one and then another false identity so that he can observe Bella as well as assist the elderly couple, the Boffins, who were kind to him as a child and who will inherit his father's fortune in his place.

The second identity John Harmon assumes is that of John Rokesmith. As Rokesmith, he takes lodging in the home of Bella's parents and goes to work for Mr. Boffin as his secretary. In this position he can both observe Bella, whom the Boffins invite to stay with them as a form of recompense for her lost prospects as young Harmon's bride, as well as oversee the new financial complexity facing the Boffins. Dickens plays the complicated situation for all it's worth, having Bella play the part of "'a widow who was never married'" (I, 4).

John discovers two things in observing Bella. The first is that he is in love with her. The second is that she appears to be a "'mercenary little wretch'" (II, 8), as she calls herself, who would have gladly married him for his money.[19] When he offers her his affections as the poor secretary, Bella turns him down, convinced that she must marry money. She is a beautiful woman with the opportunity to use her looks to obtain a comfortable marriage, and so she assumes that this is in fact what she desires.

The Boffins, however, are not convinced that she is as superficial as she judges herself to be. Nor are they fooled by Harmon's posing as Rokesmith. In a move not made completely clear to the reader until the end of the novel, the Boffins devise a plan together with Rokesmith to "test" Bella and show her her own true self as a person of principle who would refuse the wealth for love.

As the Boffin plot comes to its conclusion, we find that Bella has indeed passed every test. While the focus is on her surviving the trial of character, she is not the only character to come into her true identity. John Harmon himself must learn to trust, for it is his own mistrustfulness that leads him into the initial plan of deception.[20] It is only when he, too, can find the self that can both accept love and trust in the goodness of others that he and Bella can accept their identities as John and Bella Harmon. With Mr. Boffin also there is a change in identity. His deception in the plan to test Bella is the assumption of a miserly persona.[21] We learn of this persona through the eyes of Bella,[22] but have reason to doubt its veracity. Once John and Bella have found their true selves, Mr. Boffin is finally able to express his true identity as a benevolent man, now of means, who is the Golden Dustman, transformer of the dust mounds into gold dust.

The Lizzie–Eugene Plot Line

Alongside the development of this plot is the second story line of the novel, that concerning Lizzie Hexam and Eugene Wrayburn. As noted above, it is Gaffer Hexam who finds the body in the Thames River bearing John Harmon's identification. Shortly thereafter, Gaffer is killed while plying his trade,[23] but his memory is besmirched by the suspicion that he actually killed John Harmon. Harmon, knowing the truth of the matter, disguises himself and takes the steps necessary to clear Hexam's name once he hears of the distress that the false suspicion causes his daughter, Lizzie.

Through the course of events surrounding the discovery of the dead body and then the clearing of Hexam's name, a disaffected young barrister named Eugene Wrayburn meets Lizzie Hexam and is greatly attracted to her. When we first meet Eugene, he is attending a dinner party at the home of the Veneerings, "bran-new people in a bran-new house in a bran-new quarter of London."[24] Lest we miss the significance of their name, the narrator tells us that "in the Veneering establishment . . . all things were in a state of high varnish and polish. And what was observable in the furniture, was observable in the Veneerings—the surface smelt a little too much of the workshop and was a trifle stickey" (I, 2). The Veneering establishment serves as the home of Society, with all of its superficiality and emptiness. It is a world in which all attention is paid to externalities, none to a person's inner core.

True identity is repressed at the Veneerings, to the extent that people fail to know who they are, or who others are. People become interchangeable and indistinguishable, like the two characters known as Boots and Brewer, of whom Mr. Veneering "clearly has no distinct idea which is which." There is, we are told, "a fusion of Boots in Brewer and Brewer in Boots," such that their individual identities are totally irrelevant to Society (I, 2). The shallowness of people's claims to their personal status is also questioned by the presentation of Lady Tippins, who as the "relict of the late Sir Thomas Tippins, knighted in mistake for somebody else" (I, 10), is a false human being whose status in Society rests on an utterly false basis, though no one cares. In this environment, symbolic of the social stratification of England's class system and of the pretentiousness of the middle class in particular, most of the characters are not even aware that there is anything false about their identities. But even where the characters sense the falseness, they are literally not able to find their true identity. One such character is Twemlow, who makes the futile attempt to find genuineness in society and make sense of the social relationships. Twemlow, who is viewed as "an innocent piece of dinner-furniture," is profoundly confused by it all. As the narrator explains, "The abyss to which he could find no bottom, and from which started forth the engrossing and ever-swelling difficulty of his life, was the insoluble question whether he was Veneering's oldest friend, or newest friend" (I, 2). Twemlow cannot find any true basis for the social relationships he finds in society, nor can he even find himself fully. He is rather a man whose cheeks are "drawn in as if he had made a great effort to retire into himself some years ago, and had got so far and had never got any farther" (I, 2). Society has kept Twemlow locked in a kind of limbo where he knows enough to look for himself and what is real in relationships, but must resign himself to being disappointed in the endeavor.

This inability to discover one's own true identity is chiefly played out in the case of Eugene, a person who cannot find his true self and so cannot assert himself in any genuine way. This is made clear in his first appearance in the novel, where he is described as sitting at the Veneerings' opulent dining table, "buried alive in the back of his chair, behind a [woman's] shoulder" (I, 2). After a while he ventures a comment on a vapid bit of conversation and the narrator notes, "A reviving impression goes round the table that Eugene is coming out. An unfulfilled impression, for he goes in again" (I, 2). As a human being, Eugene is indeed buried alive behind social convention. He is unable to come out, to assert himself, because he is attempting to do so in the humanly stultifying world of the Veneerings, where individual identity and even genuine humanity are not permitted.

Regarding his attraction to Lizzie, Eugene lacks the self-knowledge necessary to be able to understand its significance for him. Throughout the novel, he struggles with his feelings for her, but is mystified by them. Even as late as the fourth book, when Eugene has become obsessed with the issue of what his intentions are toward Lizzie, he admits to himself that he is "'Not sure of myself'" (IV, 6). Deep self-knowledge is required for Eugene to discover his true desires and act upon them. Eugene's identity is so deeply concealed from him by Society's conventions, however, that only a violent rupture to his existence will allow him to discover himself.[25]

The requisite violence is supplied by Bradley Headstone,[26] the schoolmaster at the school where Lizzie has managed to send her younger and deeply ungrateful brother, Charley. Bradley also is attracted to Lizzie, and decides that he is willing to lift her up socially to the status he has achieved as a schoolmaster.[27] When she rejects his offer, he turns his passionate wrath on Eugene, who infuriates and humiliates Bradley by ignoring him, even refusing to call him by any name other than "Schoolmaster"[28] (II, 6). Eventually, Bradley's obsession with Eugene reaches the point where he stalks him. Eugene in turn taunts Bradley, spending his days plotting circuitous routes for Bradley to follow him at night. In so doing, Eugene helps bring upon himself the attack that precipitates his final acceptance of his true identity.

Throughout this drama, Lizzie is deeply distressed. As a poor young woman forced to work for her living, she is convinced that marriage between her and a person of Eugene's class is not possible. Yet she loves him. Fearing the temptation of the situation and desirous of not bringing Bradley's wrath down upon Eugene, she flees to the country near London. Eventually, Eugene tracks her down and meets with her. She begs him to leave her alone. Eugene feels the force of her plea, but cannot even assure her that he will honor her request. He says to her, "'You don't know what my state of mind towards you is. You don't know how you haunt and bewilder me. You don't know how the cursed carelessness that is over-officious in helping me at every other turning of my life, WON'T help me here. You have struck it dead, I think, and I sometimes almost wish you had struck me dead along with it'" (IV, 6).

The difficulty for Eugene here, so poignantly expressed, is that his former way of functioning in society can no longer serve him. Lizzie has awakened in him a depth of feeling that cannot be masked by an assumed identity of carelessness, but since he has not yet touched his own inner truth, he has nothing to take the place of his social identity. He is indeed not sure of himself.

Eugene continues in this bewildered state as he walks alongside the river, trying to come to some clarity about his feelings and the course he wants to pursue. Suddenly, he is murderously attacked by Bradley Headstone, falls into the river, and is left for dead. Lizzie, walking at a distance, hears the attack and then the splash. "Her old bold life and habit instantly inspired her." When she sees a body floating in the river, she prays:

> Now, merciful Heaven be thanked for that old time, and grant, O Blessed Lord, that through thy wonderful workings it may turn to good at last! To whomsoever the drifting face belongs, be it man's or be it woman's, help my humble hands, Lord God, to raise it from death and restore it to some one to whom it must be dear! (IV, 6)

Lizzie's rescue is successful. Eugene is seriously injured, his face badly disfigured but "beyond disfigurement in her eyes" (IV, 6). Gradually he recovers, with his struggle to regain and stay conscious concomitant with his struggle to discover and act from his true self. Eventually Eugene is able to express his desire to marry Lizzie. Significantly, the marriage is no miraculous cure. We are not sure if the scars of Eugene's violent death to his stultifying, socially imposed identity ever fully heal. We do know, however, that it is Lizzie who can revive him whenever he begins to slip away. As he tells her after their marriage ceremony, "'Lizzie, . . . whenever you see me wandering away from this refuge that I have so ill deserved, speak to me by my name, and I think I shall come back'" (IV, 11).

The novel closes with a scene at the Veneerings'. At yet another dinner party in the superficial world of Society, the discussion revolves around Eugene's decision to marry "'a female waterman, turned factory girl,'" with Society's repressive voice weighing in against the union. The suggestion is even made that a committee be formed to discuss "'the whole ridiculous affair'" (IV, 17). Only Eugene's friend Mortimer and the confused but good-hearted Twemlow support Eugene's marriage. The reader knows, however, that the false world of the Veneerings cannot endure the tests of life. The Veneerings themselves are about to fall, "[h]aving found out the clue to that great mystery how people can contrive to live beyond their means" (IV, 17). The voice of Society speaks from a superficial foundation. It cannot endure because it cannot understand that there needs to be something beneath the surface that grounds action. It cannot recognize that the question of Eugene's decision to marry Lizzie "'is a question of the feelings of a gentleman,'" as Twemlow puts it, not a matter for committee debate.[29] In the world of the Veneerings it is virtually impossible for a person to discover true identity and act from true feelings, but true feelings are, in the end, the only sure source of moral action in *Our Mutual Friend*.

The complex plot structure of this novel mirrors the dynamic nature of life. With the various interconnections centering on John Harmon as our mutual friend, Dickens manages to duplicate the genuine interconnectedness at the heart of existence.[30] What happens to one character in the Boffin plot can touch the lives of characters in the Lizzie-Eugene plot. The death of a riverside character presumed to be John Harmon leads to profound changes in the lives of Lizzie and Eugene, for example. Unfortunately, in the analysis that follows, it will not be possible to consider Dickens's treatment of identity in all of the main characters of the novel. For the sake of clarity, only his treatment of four characters in the Lizzie-Eugene plot will be analyzed: Lizzie Hexam, Eugene Wrayburn, Bradley Headstone, and Jenny Wren. However, it is important to keep in mind that identity is the central theme of the novel and all that Dickens accomplishes with these characters he does while exploring a multitude of nuances of this theme with other characters of the novel.

Analysis

Lizzie Hexam and the Acceptance of Particularity

The novel may end with an affirmation of a simple truth, but it begins with a recognition of complexity. This is because, to use Dyson's words, "all [Dickens] does, morally, is to tell the truth."[31] The opening scene, referred to earlier, with its depiction of Gaffer and Lizzie on the river and their different views toward it, is one that can be described as a dramatization of luck. Lizzie Hexam, like all of us, lives a situated life. She is born into a complex set of circumstances, some of which seem to compromise her morally. She loves her father dearly, yet she is appalled by his occupation. He wants her assistance, and she feels bound to provide it. Moreover, she feels that her presence effects a restraint upon her father's activities. Were she to leave him, his work might take a more questionable turn. Significantly, Lizzie does have the opportunity to break from her father's occupation without abandoning him altogether. Miss Abbey Potterson has repeatedly offered Lizzie employment at her public house, the Fellowship Porters, but Lizzie, though grateful, consistently turns the offer down. Clearly, then, Lizzie is presented as making a choice, but a highly constrained choice, to continue to assist her father, even though she feels morally compromised by his activity.

As the plot of the novel makes us see, however, it is Lizzie's task to realize that she is not compromised. Even her participation in that old occupation is not itself morally bad. Throughout the novel, Lizzie is burdened by her own harsh self-judgment and her ready acceptance of society's assessment of her and that activity. It is, however, only when *she* is able to be thankful for the occupation that she is able to act entirely out of her own self and assume her true identity.[32]

The significance of this for the meaning of the novel as a whole cannot be overstated. Lizzie is presented from the start as the most morally sensitive character in the novel. Her inner goodness is beyond question from the start. Unlike Bella, John, and Eugene, she does not need to undergo a specific test of character or change of identity. Yet she, too, must come to accept herself and the circumstances of her life without judgment. This radical self-acceptance is key. Only when it is complete is a character fully able to help others achieve their own true identity. Indeed, for all of Lizzie's goodness, she is unable to save the people initially most dear to her: her brother, Charley, and her father, Gaffer. Charley descends in his ingratitude to become a despicable fellow, and her father dies at his occupation while Lizzie is at home cooking his dinner. Dickens makes an important distinction in the manner of Gaffer's death—Gaffer's occupation kills him. Dickens's entry in the work plans for the chapter, "Kill Gaffer retributively,"[33] indicates that Dickens is still willing to pronounce a judgment. His point with Lizzie is that it does not serve *her* to judge her father. Each person must accept themselves and their lives (though not blindly) without making disabling judgments, even though aspects of their existence might be properly subject to judgment by others. But Lizzie's inability to save her family has a twofold cause. Lizzie can only help those who are in the process of actively seeking their true identity,[34] but her action is truly efficacious only after she embraces her own particular past with gratitude, as she does when rescuing Eugene. Her prayer of thanksgiving for the old days as she rows to rescue the floating body is a song of acceptance. Only now can she accept her past as well as her present place in life; only now can she accept the contingency and finitude of existence, which make her life the particular life that it is.

The importance of this acceptance is made clear by her success in the rescue attempt, but it is also underscored by the change in Lizzie herself. Prior to this moment, she feels the social chasm between herself and Eugene every bit as much as Society itself does, and she is paralyzed by it. In her words to

Eugene shortly before the attack, in which she implores him to leave her, she communicates a complete acceptance of social stratification: "'Think of me, as belonging to another station, and quite cut off from you in honour.'" And again, "'I am removed from you and your family by being a working girl'" (IV, 6). In this section she is concerned to protect her reputation and is asking Eugene to respect her wishes because she is convinced that nothing could ever come of any relationship between them. It is true that Eugene's indecisiveness exacerbates the situation for her, but it is also true that she needs to step out from the shadow of not only her past but also her station to act fully as a human being. Only after her prayer of acceptance and the rescue does she act freely out of her identity as one who loves Eugene. Once she makes her own self-accepting act, she no longer hides behind her station. She visits Eugene freely over a period of time *before* he asks her to marry him. She is not dependent on Eugene's self-awareness in his decision to marry her for her own freedom to act out of her heart toward him. Full self-acceptance is as liberating for her as it is for him.

Dickens's treatment of Lizzie is far from simple, however. In her, he depicts a character who finds herself born into circumstances that both she and society find morally compromising, yet he also presents her as a character who chooses loyalty to a father over the appearance of moral purity and reputation. In Lizzie, he intends us to see a truly good person. In all of her dealings with people, she is upright and straightforward. Dickens has been criticized for giving her too refined a diction for a person of her circumstances,[35] but this gentleness of speech is meant to convey her gentleness of soul. The key indication that Lizzie is regarded in an exceptionally good light is her ability to "read stories" and see into the future in the fire. In Dickens's novels, and in this novel in particular, this gift of vision is associated with goodness.[36] What is interesting is that in his characterization of Lizzie he also shows the ambiguous nature of life and the effect that this ambiguity has on her. She knows instinctively, it seems, that solipsistic moral purity is not the moral high road in her situation. She also seems to know that there is no one path that will cancel all of the ambiguity, even if it is not, technically speaking, moral ambiguity. Her task in the novel is to accept even this ambiguity, exchanging her shame over her father's past activity and her complicity in it for gratitude. For most of the novel, she is not able to do this. She instead continues with her own quiet dignity to go on with her life, but always, it seems, in the shadow of this past activity. Dickens makes it clear to us that she has committed no moral wrong in deciding to help her father. But he also makes it clear that she is limited by her inability to accept her past. At one point, she tells her brother Charley that she almost cannot get away from the river. She seeks to perform some kind of recompense for "'Father's grave'" (II, 1).[37] But her father's past is not hers to redeem. She needs to accept him as she accepts herself, and not use his activity as an excuse to hide from her own fullness.[38]

If Lizzie's situation with her father is not a case of moral luck in the sense considered in chapter 3, it does highlight the depth of vulnerability in life. Here we have Lizzie, a truly good person,[39] who is placed in a difficult position solely by another person, her father. Though her moral task of self-acceptance would seem to be straightforward, the conditions of her life make this task difficult. After her father's death, she must deal with the suspicion that he had committed the Harmon murder, something that colors both his memory and her own reputation. Beyond that, she has an ungrateful brother, an unsure suitor in Eugene and an obviously unstable one in Bradley Headstone, and the need to work to support herself. Lizzie's goodness does not clear a path for her. Life's obstacles are ever present as she tries to find her way to peace and love. Moreover, other characters in the novel have more propitious circumstances for their own journeys to full identity and acceptance of self. Bella, for example, "is tested not in the furnace of life like . . . Lizzie Hexam, but in the play of Boffin's golden affection and love."[40] What Dickens captures in creating this diversity of conditions is the very real phenomenon that "[s]ome people have all the luck."[41]

Eugene Wrayburn and Self-Discovery

Dickens is also true to life in showing each character's task of self-acceptance as unique. In Eugene's case, we see a man who must do more than accept the ambiguous aspects of a particular life, as Lizzie does. What Eugene must do is discover himself. In his depiction of Eugene Wrayburn, Dickens clearly indicates an underlying anthropology that asserts that we are more than what happens to us, that we have an inner core and true identity that is ours alone and that we must claim. Eugene's task is not an historical retelling of his past so that he can become his own judge, as Rorty sees the fundamental act of freedom,[42] nor is he called to create the truth about himself.[43] Instead, he needs to discover the truth about himself, about who he is as a person.[44] From his birth, he has led a life in which someone else has created his identity, first his father and, later, Society itself.[45] His father, he tells his good friend Mortimer, has found a woman for him to marry. She comes from "'the parental neighborhood'" and has some money. Eugene goes on to explain his situation to Mortimer:

"M. R. F. [my respected father] having always in the clearest manner provided (as he calls it) for his children by pre-arranging from the hour of the birth of each, and sometimes from an earlier period, what the devoted little victim's calling and course in life should be, M. R. F. pre-arranged for myself that I was to be the barrister I am (with the slight addition of an enormous practice, which has not accrued), and also the married man that I am not." (I, 12)

Eugene's father has exercised total control over the lives of his children, appointing one to run the family estate, one to the church, another to the sea, and yet another to engineering. At marriage, however, Eugene draws the line, though in a vague, nonassertive way, objecting not to the woman herself, whom he has never seen, nor to his father's role in finding her, but to the idea of marriage, on the grounds that he is too easily bored.[46] What we should not fail to see, however, is that in rejecting rather than accepting this aspect of his externally created identity, Eugene is beginning to resist his false identity.

At this point in his life Eugene is leading the most passive of existences. He has a career he has not chosen and to which he does not apply himself, he attends social events he does not like, and he finds his life on the whole boring. The only deliberate act of his life is not to care about anything. This carelessness, which later fails him, is his chosen stance toward life.[47] With his identity as a professional and a member of the middle class, he moves in a certain social world, one that includes the Veneerings and Lady Tippins. He does not invest any passion in his social engagements, yet he allows this façade of a social life to pass for the real thing. Then he meets Lizzie and, to use Jennifer Gribble's words, he feels some "inner promptings" that are "at odds with his social identity."[48] Gradually he turns toward Lizzie, offering to provide her and her friend Jenny Wren with some schooling. But his lifelong passivity makes his discovery of his true identity difficult, despite the inner promptings. With Eugene, Dickens illustrates the difficulty of casting off a social identity that provides a certain ease of life. As a member of the middle class, Eugene, whose name, it has been pointed out, suggests good breeding,[49] has a passport to all that the middle class has to offer. He has the makings of a respectable career, the certainty of social invitations, and marital eligibility. In many respects, he is a winner in the natural lottery. Yet Dickens helps us see through the façade. No matter what one's luck in life, it is always destructive merely to resign oneself to what one is given. What must be actively accepted is one's own true self, the one touched by inner promptings, the self that one *is*. This self is characterized by deep limitation and dependency, but it is clearly more than merely finite and contingent. As such, self-acceptance involves accepting the givenness of life for what it is—one's initial place in life—but it also involves not merely resigning oneself to this.[50]

In Eugene's case, he has so buried himself in his socially conferred identity that he cannot find himself by himself. Significantly, he does make the moves that he can in response to his inner promptings. He responds to Lizzie, and although he does not understand the magnitude of his feelings he honors them by seeking to help her. He also recognizes that there is something destructive about his inability to find himself. We sense this in his relationship with Bradley Headstone. Their conversations are filled with tension. Eugene knows that he is playing a dangerous game in taunting Bradley by leading him on wild goose chases night after night, but he continues nonetheless. He presents this act to himself and his friend Mortimer[51] as merely a diversion from his boredom, but in the level of intensity with which he undertakes this act we find the first sign of passion in Eugene. It is as if he is drawn to the violent rupture of his surface identity so that his true self can emerge from the wreckage.

That Eugene cannot accomplish his most basic task alone illustrates the degree to which Dickens sees our dependence upon others. The interconnectedness is highlighted by the fact that Eugene's act of self-discovery is dependent upon both Bradley's rage and Lizzie's old occupation (just as Lizzie's is dependent on his need to be rescued). As basic as this task is, it cannot be accomplished alone. With Eugene, this dependency is particularly dramatic, but it is a manifestation of what Dickens takes to be a basic aspect of existence. Dickens in fact reiterates this need to rely upon others in Eugene's period of recovery. After Bradley's murderous attack upon him, Eugene barely survives. In the period that follows, Eugene is depicted as constantly wavering between consciousness and unconsciousness. These two states obviously represent his grasping of his identity and losing it. Eugene himself refers to his slipping away as "'los[ing] myself again'" (IV, 10). During his recuperation, Eugene develops a deep desire that he cannot articulate. He is again dependent, first on Jenny Wren to discover that what he wants is to marry Lizzie,[52] and then on Mortimer to make all of the arrangements. Once married, he relies upon Lizzie to call him back to himself whenever he fades.

Eugene's state of dependency as the novel closes has received criticism.[53] He is depicted as suffering the scars of his fight and having a diminished consciousness. However, as to the bleakness itself, the novel is actually quite open. There are hints that Eugene may sparkle as he grows stronger and that his disfigurement will be less noticeable.[54] He has the prospect of a flourishing partnership with Mortimer, whose career truly takes off by the end of the novel. He also now has the courage to face Society's judgment of his marriage to Lizzie, and we have every reason to hope that, in a world peopled with not just the Veneerings but also the Harmons and the Boffins, his courage will be rewarded. We already know that his father has accepted the marriage, offering what Eugene says is "'equivalent to a melodramatic blessing'" (IV, 16).[55] Eugene is not a shadow of a man. He was that at the start of the novel, though he may have cut a dashing figure then.[56] Yet despite these hopeful possibilities, *Our Mutual Friend* is no romantic fairy tale. It tells the truth about existence, and that truth is that we are vulnerable beings and that life's circumstances can indeed be bad for us. Moreover, the marks of the damage we incur are not completely erased, not even by love, though it may be the most regenerative force available to us.[57] Just as moral goodness does not clear a path of ease for Lizzie, so, too, the claiming of his true identity in the act of accepting love does not erase all of the scars of Eugene's life. We do not know the extent of the limitations to his healing, but we know enough to surmise that they are significant. What is key is that Eugene can now live fully because in his active acceptance of himself as the one who loves Lizzie, and of her love for him, crystallized in their marriage, he truly becomes a free man.[58] Eugene will always be dependent upon Lizzie, for it is in his active acceptance of his love for her that he is able to be who he truly is. Likewise, Lizzie will always be dependent upon Eugene. Saving him will always be the act that allows her to embrace the particularities of her existence, and loving him will always be how she acts as her true self. But accepting this in no way diminishes either Eugene or Lizzie, for it is the acceptance of limitation that liberates.

Bradley Headstone and Self-Repression

While in Eugene we have a character who, having passively accepted a superficial social identity, must discover his true identity, in Bradley Headstone, his counterpart,[59] we have a character who consistently represses his true self, desperately seeking to sustain a socially acceptable identity.[60] Through an explicit focus on Bradley's identity as a schoolmaster, Dickens shows us the cost to a person of denying the full range of one's truth, a range that includes one's birth, one's situation, and one's temperament. Dickens lets us see that what Bradley cannot accept is his own particularity, the givenness of his life. We perceive this most acutely in his relationship with Eugene, right from the start. When he first meets Eugene, he mistakenly assumes that Eugene has made a judgment about his past. In a pathetic display of his insecurity surrounding his place in life, he demands of Eugene,

> "Do you throw my obscurity in my teeth, Mr. Wrayburn?"
>
> "That can hardly be, for I know nothing concerning it, Schoolmaster, and seek to know nothing."
>
> "You reproach me with my origin," said Bradley Headstone; "you cast insinuations at my bringing-up. But I tell you, sir, I have worked my way onward, out of both and in spite of both, and have a right to be considered a better man than you, with better reasons for being proud." (II, 6)

In the conversation that precedes this exchange, Eugene has been maddeningly insolent to Bradley, totally controlling the situation. He has not, however, made any reference to Bradley's "'origin'" or "'bringing-up.'" This topic arises solely with Bradley. As his words to Eugene indicate, however, he has been obsessed with overcoming his particular place in life. He has struggled to obtain the socially acceptable identity of schoolmaster, not as a way of realizing his true self but as a way of hiding his own reality, even from himself. Even when Eugene asks his name, he refuses at first to give it, telling him only his profession. His sole desire is to be identified as the respectable schoolmaster. During the course of the conversation, he realizes that this title is not commanding the respect from Eugene to which he feels entitled, for instead of using the title respectfully, Eugene uses it dismissively. The increasingly frustrated Bradley, in his effort to show his depth as a human being, reveals much. "'Do you suppose,'" he says to Eugene, "'that a man, in forming himself for the duties I discharge, and in watching and repressing himself daily to discharge them well, dismisses a man's nature?'" To which Eugene responds, "'I suppose you . . . judging from what I see as I look at you, to be rather too passionate for a good schoolmaster'" (II, 6). Eugene scores a telling blow, for he sees instantly that the identity that Bradley has worked so hard to earn from society does not match his nature. While Bradley deems it to his credit that he has repressed himself, Eugene points out the obvious: he has devoted himself to acquiring an identity that simply does not fit him. He is trying to be someone other than who he is. Bradley's approach toward life is intentionally self-destructive in that it seeks to deny his true identity. This way of living can only end in complete self-destruction.

To the reader, Eugene's observation is a reiteration, for the narrator has already called attention to Bradley's unsuitableness for his career and identity. When Bradley first appears in the novel, the narrator observes,

> Bradley Headstone, in his decent black coat and waistcoat and decent white shirt, and decent formal black tie, and decent pantaloons of pepper and salt . . . looked a thoroughly decent young man of six-and-twenty. He was never seen in any other dress, and yet there was a certain stiffness in his manner of wearing this, as if there were a want of adaption between him and it. . . .
>
> Suppression of so much to make room for so much, had given him a constrained manner, over and above. Yet there was enough of what was animal, and of what was fiery (though smouldering), still visible in him, to suggest that if young Bradley Headstone, when a pauper lad, had chanced to be off for the sea, he would not have been the last man in a ship's crew. Regarding that origin of his, he was proud, moody, and sullen, desiring it to be forgotten. (II, 1)

There is a certain want of fit between the clothes, which are the outward signs of a particular identity and the man who wears them. In his creation of Bradley Headstone, Dickens illustrates vibrantly that the problem is not in the pauper lad himself, nor in the garb of a schoolmaster, but in the fit. Bradley has chosen a career expressly to hide his true self from the world, not to bring it to fruition. Such a grand deception cannot succeed. In a less passionate nature such a failure would have taken a different form perhaps, but in Bradley it is explosive. In a brilliant psychological statement, Dickens shows us the intensity of Bradley's position by juxtaposing him with Eugene, a character who wants to cast off the enviable identity society has bestowed on him. We feel Bradley's rage at the seeming injustice of it all, and strangely sympathize with him as his hatred for Eugene grows.[61] Ultimately, Bradley's own nature, repressed daily though it may be, burns through the straightjacket he has outfitted himself with, to the point where he attempts to murder Eugene and finally destroys himself. That he is in fact destroyed is presented in a quiet but dramatic move. As the intricacies of Bradley's attack on Eugene close in on him, he "turned his face to the black board and slowly wiped his name out" (IV, 15).[62] His suicide the next day is at this point inevitable. Bradley cannot exist when it is no longer possible for the schoolmaster to exist. His attempt to hide his true identity thus results in his own destruction[63] and Eugene's severe injury. The potential ramifications reach further than this, for had he succeeded in killing Eugene he would also have killed the man Lizzie loved and Mortimer's best friend. The cost to self and others is clearly great when a person tries to reject his or her self and assume a false and misfitting identity.

Yet here again Dickens is a master at displaying realistically the ambiguity of life. As it happens, Bradley's explosive attack on Eugene brings about not only his own end but also a new beginning for Eugene. Dickens knows that the nature of the interdependency of life is not simple. What is destructive for one can be creative for another, though still retaining some destructive elements. Eugene and Lizzie both depend on Bradley's self-destruction (which is anything but self-giving) for their own full self-acceptance.[64] Dickens provides no clue as to whether or not their personal development could have occurred in a less destructive way. Instead he merely tells the truth, that what is "bad" for one person can be "good" for another, and such is the nature of existence.

Jenny Wren: Vulnerability and Self-Acceptance

Throughout the novel, Dickens offers several variations on his theme of acceptance of one's self through his treatment of identity. This analysis concentrates on the characters from the Lizzie-Eugene plot, but each of the main characters of the Boffin plot also reveals a facet of Dickens's understanding of the importance of accepting one's identity and the conditions of one's life for living an authentic human life.[65] Dickens's treatment of his theme is thus multifaceted. Against this backdrop there is one character, however, who shines as the gem of the novel, the one in whom Dickens brings together the key facets of his overall theme. This character is the doll's dressmaker, Jenny Wren. She is a relatively minor character who figures mainly in the Lizzie-Eugene plot, linking up with a character from the Boffin plot only at the end.[66] But in her we have a fine and complete depiction of the central issue of the novel. She alone shows both the degree of our vulnerability and the possibilities of efficacy that come from acceptance of self and the particularities of one's life.

Jenny enters the novel just a few pages after the narrator has informed us of Bradley's unsuitableness for the identity he has chosen for suppressing his true self, juxtaposing her stance toward her identity with Bradley's. Charley Hexam and Bradley have come to Jenny's home looking for Lizzie, who boards with Jenny now that Gaffer is dead. Jenny is introduced thus: "A parlour door within a small entry stood open, and disclosed a child—a dwarf— a girl—a something—sitting on a little low old-fashioned arm-chair, which had a kind of little working bench before it." In response to a knock at the door, she calls out, "'I can't get up . . . because my back's bad, and my legs are queer. But I'm the person of the house'" (II, 1). With Jenny, we have none of Bradley's repression. Nor do we have Eugene's resignation, nor even Lizzie's ambivalence. No, she knows who she is, and she claims her identity. She is the person of the house, with a bad back and queer legs.

In his depiction of Jenny, Dickens also gives us a poignant picture of human vulnerability. Jenny is physically disfigured, such that one cannot even tell her age.[67] Her disfigurement has caused her great emotional pain from the inevitable teasing by other children, to the point where she prefers only the company of adults[68] and the peaceful beauty of her imaginary flowers and birds.[69] Her mother is dead and her father is an alcoholic in the terminal stages of his disease who dies before the end of the novel. (She in fact comes from a line of alcoholics, with her grandfather, whose corpse Gaffer had robbed, having also been an alcoholic.)[70] As is so often the case in a Dickens novel, and in life itself, the neglected child becomes the parent. In this case, the role reversal is explicit, with Jenny referring to her father as her child, her "'bad child'" (III, 2). Dickens is brutally honest in his portrayal of her situation. As the narrator explains,

> The person of the house was the person of a house full of sordid shames and cares, with an upper room in which that abased figure [her father] was infecting even innocent sleep with sensual brutality and degradation. The doll's dressmaker had become a little quaint shrew; of the world, worldly; of the earth, earthy. (II, 2)

Her shrewness manifests itself in her frequent elaborations of the cruel treatment she would give a real or fictitious person. However, rather than to condemn Jenny for the free reign she gives her imagination, there is good reason to see her penchant for cruel expressions as part of the harm she has suffered. Surely her capacity for cruel imaginings grew in proportion to the cruelty she experienced. Significantly, on only one occasion does she actually do something that could be described as cruel, and it is something that also could be described as giving someone his just deserts.[71] Jenny knows what it is to feel pain and to contemplate giving pain, but she is not herself a cruel person.

As we come to know more of Jenny, we learn that she was born Fanny Cleaver, but had given herself the name Jenny Wren long ago. In her case, this self-naming is an act of claiming her true identity, not avoiding it.[72] Dickens stresses the aptness of her renaming herself by noting that her sparkling eye, the symbol of her perspicacity, is as "bright and watchful as the bird's whose name she had taken" (II, 11). Indeed, throughout the novel, what sets Jenny apart is her ability to see the truth. Sylvia Bank Manning has correctly observed that she is "the touchstone of truth" in the novel.[73] Her vision, however, like her whole being, is sharp. Her insight has none of the softness of Lizzie's that comes from reading pictures in the fire. No, her perspicacity is immediate and unsparing.[74] Her ability to see through the falseness and inhumanity of the world is striking.

This sharpness of vision may have its origin in what appears to be instinct; Jenny no doubt possesses a natural ability to see clearly where others cannot. But we cannot escape the view that her ability has been honed by the trials of her life. In order to survive, Jenny has had to recognize the reality of her situation from an early age. She is the crippled child of an alcoholic. Further, she has been exposed mainly to the cruel side of children, so play and companionship have been denied her. She has had to see, as a child, that she is the person of the house, the one on whom she and her father must depend. She has had to cope with her physical limitations. And she has had to find her own comforts in life, apart from the normal joys of childhood. That she has recognized her responsibilities and limitations, and has accepted them in order to function, is portrayed beautifully for us in one brief passage. Jenny and her friend Riah, an elderly Jew in the employ of a duplicitous money lender, are leaving her home:

> Satisfied that her dwelling was safe, she drew one hand through the old man's arm and prepared to ply her crutch-stick with the other. But the key was an instrument of such gigantic proportions, that before they started Riah proposed to carry it.
>
> "No, no, no! I'll carry it myself," returned Miss Wren. "I'm awfully lopsided, you know, and stowed down in my pocket it'll trim the ship. To let you into a secret, godmother, I wear my pocket on my high side, o' purpose."[75] (III, 2)

This is how Jenny actively accepts her life. Her burdensome domestic responsibilities, symbolized by the key of "gigantic proportions," are used to balance, not exacerbate, her physical disability. She uses the key to "trim the ship," and has sewn her pocket where this can be accomplished. There is a sense of pride and cheerfulness about this young woman-child, who can bring the disquieting aspects of her life so effectively into balance.

As with Eugene and Lizzie, however, Dickens gives us no simple romantic picture of good triumphing over evil. Jenny's life contains inordinate pain. She is consistently portrayed as engaged in struggle. Both her disability and her home life weigh heavily on her. Yet she endures and even thrives. Her occupation, in which she revels, again shows her pragmatic drive to function. As she and Riah continue on their walk, they pass a toy-shop window filled with an array of dolls, which causes Jenny to exclaim, "'Now look at 'em! All my work!'" To Riah's compliments she responds, "'Glad you like 'em. . . . But the fun is, godmother, how I make the great ladies try my dresses on.'" Riah does not immediately understand her words, so Jenny explains that she puts the women of high society to work for her as models. She describes a typical situation in which she finds a model, goes home to cut the pattern out, and returns at a later time to check the accuracy of her work. Turning the tables completely around, she, the poor doll's dressmaker, "employs" the woman of high society, "'making a perfect slave of her,'" as Jenny puts it (III, 2). In this act, Jenny shows her two salient traits: perspicacity and efficaciousness. She sees the women, devoted to society, for what they are—mere mannequins— and she creatively uses what she alone perceives in order to make a living for herself. No doubt her occupation also satisfies her desire to enjoy dolls, one of the pleasures of childhood, albeit in a very adult way. Jenny thus at once sees reality and is not stymied by what she sees. When Lizzie sees the middle and upper class, she sees a barrier to herself. When Eugene sees society, he sees a convenient identity. Bradley sees an identity to hide behind. Jenny alone sees clearly the falseness and inhumanity of the social structure, but accepts what she finds and uses it effectively for her own creative purposes.[76]

Jenny's acceptance of both herself and the circumstances of her life is complete. Unlike the other characters discussed above, she has no central task to accomplish in the novel.[77] In showing Jenny's ability to thrive in such overwhelming circumstances, Dickens evinces a faith in the ability of human beings to flourish, regardless of their situation, if only they will face it honestly and acceptingly. But hers is not an easy acceptance. One could hardly accept her life genuinely without struggle and pain. Moreover, she accepts not just the particular features of her own life, but the conditions of life itself. In a scene with Lizzie, Riah, and Fascination Fledgeby on the rooftop of Pubsey and Co., where Riah fronts Fledgeby's loan business, Jenny describes the peace and comfort she experiences up above the city. She likens the experience of being up high to being dead:

> "Ah!" said Jenny. "But it's so high. And you see the clouds rushing on above the narrow streets, not minding them, and you see the golden arrows pointing at the mountains in the sky from which the wind comes, and you feel as if you were dead."

Fledgeby then asks her how it feels to be dead.

> "Oh, so tranquil!" cried the little creature, smiling. "Oh, so peaceful and so thankful! And you hear the people who are alive, crying, and working, and calling to one another down in the close dark streets, and you seem to pity them so! And such a chain has fallen from you, and such a strange good sorrowful happiness comes upon you!" (II, 5)

Fledgeby resists her view, grumbling. To this Jenny sharply replies, "'But *you* are not dead, you know. . . . Get down to life!'"

This passage has been read as an example of escapism, evidence that Jenny deals immaturely with death.[78] Indeed the first paragraph quoted lends itself to that view. She does describe an ethereal state that offers peace and comfort. But the second paragraph, and her response to Fledgeby's grumbling, suggest greater depth. Dickens shows in Jenny an understanding of life that has two dimensions. The first involves a reversal of the two worlds. In the life below, life dictated by society's falseness, to die is to be truly alive. Those who can come up and be dead are those who can truly live.[79] Jenny sees immediately that Fledgeby cannot do this. His life revolves around the falsity of society, for he makes his living loaning money to those who attempt to transcend their limitations by living beyond their means. His rejection of Jenny's view amounts to a denial of real finitude in an attempt to prolong the delusion that is life in society.[80]

The second dimension this interchange points to connects with a recurrent theme in the novel: resurrection. Throughout the novel, characters experience a kind of death or suspension of life, as Eugene does, out of which they emerge their true selves.[81] John Harmon, for example, in his assumed identity as John Rokesmith, finally resurrects as John Harmon, shed of the mistrust that characterized him before his "death" in the river. Bella, too, must let her old view of herself as mercenary die so that she can become her true self. Repeatedly in the novel, people who are caught in false identities must be willing to let these false selves and all of the values and concerns related to them die in order to return to the world as their true selves. Each person must be willing to come up and be dead, accept their limitations, even their mortality, to truly live. "'Come up and be dead'" is an invitation to embrace one's mortality in order to be freed of the chains of life, which otherwise weigh one down.

Acceptance

This truth that Jenny sees is, finally, the existential truth that Dickens asks us to see. Joseph Gold, in his conclusion to *Charles Dickens: Radical Moralist*, says of Dickens's canon as a whole, which culminates in *Our Mutual Friend,*

> The movement is from images of goodness, from Cheeryble philanthropy, to a disciplined self-knowledge and understanding. Indeed, Dickens comes to question whether real goodness, the redemption of the individual first and his compassion for others thereafter, is possible without the quest for the truth about oneself and unless the truth about oneself encompasses the recognition that one must die.[82]

Dickens presents this view to us in terms of identity. He shows us in character after character the need to accept our true selves, in all of our particularities, in all of our limitations. Dickens presents acceptance as a dynamic task, for it is self-acceptance that grounds future moral action and makes it possible for characters to continue to develop themselves creatively. He also stresses that this acceptance must include an acceptance of those around us, especially our families. At the heart of this acceptance, however, is an acceptance of life itself, life as contingent and finite.[83] Our particularities, which include all of those people and things on which we depend, are manifestations of the condition of existence here called contingency. Our limitations, even the limit to our mortal life, are aspects of our finitude. In his characterization of Jenny Wren, Dickens highlights what he says through all of the main characters of the novel: that we must accept, actively and fully, who we are as human beings, both who we are as particular selves and the nature of life itself, lived contingently and finitely. Genuine acceptance of ourselves is ultimately an acceptance of existence,[84] and this radical acceptance is a precursor to effective action in the world. Jenny Wren, who is so completely accepting, is the novel's example of simple effectiveness. Lizzie Hexam, undoubtedly good from the start, is only able to genuinely help others when she has accomplished this radical self-acceptance. Eugene can only truly live once he is able to discover and accept himself. And Bradley Headstone can succeed only at killing himself when his repression of his real identity fails. With his consistent focus on identity, Dickens explores his theme of acceptance of ourselves as unique but vulnerable beings in a world of great interconnectedness.[85] We are vulnerable to what others do to us, as Jenny is to her alcoholic father, as Eugene is to Bradley's rage. We are also vulnerable to what others do for us, as Eugene is to Lizzie's rescue, as Lizzie is to Eugene's need. Thus we bear the twin power to hurt and help each other. If we want to be fully responsible actors in this interconnected world, if we want to activate our power to help more than our ability to hurt, then we must fully accept ourselves and the conditions of our existence. The truth of *Our Mutual Friend* is that it is only once we accept ourselves as we are, with all that encompasses, that we are able to act efficaciously in the world.

Our Mutual Friend thus dramatizes the central task of each individual for effective action, which relates directly to our nature as beings who are deeply vulnerable to our conditions of existence. But it does not explicitly address how we are to understand our obligations to one another in terms of these conditions of existence. This is a pressing concern for us all, with a particular meaning for Christians who understand themselves to be obligated to others but are often at a loss to determine specifically how to fulfill this obligation in particular situations. Yet if Dickens is right that deep acceptance of ourselves as the beings that we are, beings who are contingent and finite each in our particular way, is a central task that must precede efficacious action, then acceptance is likely also to be the starting point for understanding better the nature of our obligations to one another and to ourselves, as well as for suggesting how we can identify what our obligations entail in concrete situations. With this in mind, it is time to turn to the primary moral task of active acceptance, to see how it helps us determine the content of our specific obligations to ourselves and others.

Notes

1. A. E. Dyson provides support for this assessment when he says of Dickens, "All that he shows of humanity seems consistent with Christian doctrine." A. E. Dyson, *The Inimitable Dickens: A Reading of the Novels* (New York: St. Martin's, 1970), 263.

2. Edgar Johnson, for example, observes that Dickens insists that "if society in many ways shapes the individual, the individual may also remold society." Edgar Johnson, *Charles Dickens: His Tragedy and Triumph*, 2 vols. (New York: Simon & Schuster, 1952), 1045.

3. Caddy Jellyby and Jo in *Bleak House* and Stephen Blackpool in *Hard Times* are examples from earlier novels. In this novel, Jenny Wren is the triumphant example of personal integrity surviving poverty, disfigurement, and neglect.

4. Dyson, *Inimitable Dickens*, 260. Dyson also observes that, in this novel, Charley and Lizzie Hexam have the same start in life, the same burdens, but very different moral characters.

5. A possible exception to this occurs early in his corpus. Although Dickens was concerned to show good triumphing over evil in *Oliver Twist* (he said in his preface to the novel's 3d edition, "I wished to show, in little Oliver, the principle of Good surviving through every adverse circumstance, and triumphing at last"; quoted in J. Hillis Miller, *Charles Dickens: The World of His Novels* [Bloomington: Indiana University Press, 1969], 36), it is clearly Oliver's bloodline and Nancy's courageous efforts that allow Oliver to triumph, not his own goodness *per se*. Compare Oliver's fate with that of another good child, Dick, who dies a victim to social evil in spite of his goodness.

6. Dyson, *Inimitable Dickens*, 260.

7. Otto Rank, *Modern Education: A Critique of Its Fundamental Ideas* (New York: Agathon, 1968), 13, quoted by Ernest Becker, *The Denial of Death* (New York: Free Press, 1973), 62. Both Dickens and Rank examine the extreme point to which we can take the fact that we need some limitation in order to act. See also William Lynch, *Images of Hope* (Baltimore: Helicon, 1965), 58, 72.

8. For example, Bella Wilfer is transformed as Bella Harmon, as Eugene is transformed after being attacked. Other characters, such as Lizzie Hexam, change less dramatically, but their change centers on finally accepting themselves fully.

9. Miller, *Charles Dickens*, 279.

10. This is not to say that all features of our existence are completely neutral. Jenny Wren's father's alcoholism is clearly destructive, and Dickens pulls no punches on this. (On the harm done to Jenny, see Dyson, *Inimitable Dickens*, 265–66.) Although her father's alcoholism is not neutral, it is also not wholly determinative. Jenny is able to accept it as a fact of her life. She is depicted as accepting this fact in her own way, so that she is able to live without being completely damaged by it. For her act of self-definition, it is important that she see that she has a choice in how she regards the alcoholism: as an evil that ruins her life or as an aspect of her existence. In taking the latter course, she is able to move beyond it as a human being and not be permanently limited by it.

11. See discussions by Edmund Wilson, "Dickens: The Two Scrooges," in *The Wound and the Bow* (Boston: Houghton Mifflin, 1941), 75–76, and H. M. Daleski, *Dickens and the Art of Analogy* (London: Faber and Faber, 1970), 276–300.

12. John Lucas, "In Conclusion: *Our Mutual Friend*," in *The Melancholy Man* (London: Methuen, 1980), 340.

13. It is a mark of Dickens's genius that he succeeded in showing the neutrality of the dust mounds to the readers of his day, who unlike us would have known the likely makeup of the mounds—part treasure perhaps, but mostly home refuse, including the contents of chamber pots. See Humphry House, *The Dickens World*, 2d ed. (New York: Oxford University Press, 1960), 166–67.

14. Charles Dickens, *Our Mutual Friend* (New York: Bantam, 1990), book I, chapter 1. All future references will be to the novel's parts, in the form of (book, chapter).

15. Dickens explicitly connects the events of the two chapters in his notes for the latter chapter in his number plans. See Michael Cotsell, *The Companion to "Our Mutual Friend"* (Boston: Allen & Unwin, 1986), 255.

16. Readers often find the plot in *Bleak House* complicated, but it is less so than it appears. Dickens achieves this effect with his use of two narrators, Esther Summerson and the "Roving Conductor" (to use Albert J. Guerard's memorable moniker, from his afterword to *Bleak House* [New York: Holt, Rinehart and Winston, 1970], 836). Dickens's aim in the novel is in part to show how simple things become complicated, and his narrative technique reflects this.

17. In a remarkably creative article, Gregg Hecimovich points out that the reader is drawn into the process of discovering identity by the very title of the novel, for the identity of our mutual friend is not "revealed" to us until the ninth chapter. His refreshing article also claims an epistemological significance for the title of book I, "The Cup and the Lip." See Gregg Hecimovich, "The Cup and the Lip and the Riddle of *Our Mutual Friend*," *English Literary History* 62 (1995): 955–77.

18. Dickens has fun with keeping the exact location a mystery, as Mortimer Lightwood tells the tale of "The Man from Somewhere," as chapter 2 (book I) is entitled.

19. John himself observes of her that she is "So insolent, so trivial, so capricious, so mercenary. . . . And yet so pretty, so pretty!" (I, 16).

20. On mistrustfulness as "the quality in himself that he must . . . conquer," see Lewis Horne, "*Our Mutual Friend* and the Test of Worthiness," *Dalhousie Review* 62, no. 2 (1982): 295–96.

21. The deception is termed a "pious fraud" in the denouement scene (IV, 13).

22. Dickens introduces us to Boffin's change in personality through the eyes of Bella, whom he wants to deceive, not through the words of the narrator. In his number plan for III, 4, he double underlines his intention to break the news of the change through Bella. See Cotsell, *Companion*, 195.

23. He is actually strangled by his own rope as he hangs over the edge of the boat trying to get hold of a corpse. The reader cannot miss that Gaffer, while he may have seen some respectability in his occupation, used the river in an inappropriate way and so suffers as a result.

24. Sylvia Bank Manning aptly puts it when she describes the Veneerings as "organic forms of nonlife." Sylvia Bank Manning, "Modified Satire: *Our Mutual Friend*," in *Dickens as Satirist* (New Haven, Conn.: Yale University Press, 1971), 203.

25. Daleski concurs that, although Eugene had begun to change before the moment of violence, it is a crisis that "forces him to complete the change." Daleski, *Dickens and the Art of Analogy*, 311. However, Daleski misses Eugene's role in bringing about the attack.

26. Dickens considered naming him Bradley Deadstone, as evidenced in his chapter plans. See plans to chapter 1 of book II in Cotsell, *Companion*, 129.

27. Joseph Gold correctly observes that Bradley's pride rather than heart is wounded by Lizzie's refusal of his offer. His social identity is offended. Joseph Gold, *Charles Dickens: Radical Moralist* (Minneapolis: University of Minnesota Press, 1972), 269.

28. Of course, Bradley had first introduced himself to Eugene as Charley's schoolmaster, giving the respectable identity he had earned from society (II, 6).

29. House reads in Twemlow's comments an acceptance of existing class structure. If this be true, then it is certainly a class structure transformed by respect for genuine feeling. See House, *Dickens World*, 163.

30. See Lucas, "In Conclusion," 342–43.

31. Dyson, *Inimitable Dickens*, 263.

32. After romantically protesting that he is not good enough for Lizzie, Eugene acknowledges that she has assumed her true identity in marrying him, saying, "But you have followed the treasure of your heart" (IV, 11).

33. Cotsell, *Companion*, 91.

34. For example, she is able to help Bella by seeing in the fire that Bella will bear all for the man she loves, thereby encouraging her toward Rokesmith. Dickens's note in his work plan, "Lizzie to work an influence on Bella's character, at its wavering point," underlined twice, indicates his intention that Lizzie's "seeing" actually helps Bella (Cotsell, *Companion*, 214). Note, however, that at this point Bella is working toward her own transformation (III, 9).

35. Daleski criticizes Dickens on this point, disagreeing with the poetic interpretation. Daleski, *Dickens and the Art of Analogy*, 307–8.

36. In *Bleak House*, for example, Esther Summerson has the ability to see what needs to be done for others, in a novel where such vision is hard to come by. In *Our Mutual Friend*, other examples of vision and goodness coming together are Mr. Bof-

fin, who sees that Bella is good inside; Mrs. Boffin, who recognizes John Harmon in Rokesmith; and Jenny Wren, who sees just about everything, and is discussed below. Of course, not all good characters possess some special visionary powers.

37. In this instance, she chooses to live with a young girl, Jenny Wren, whose grandfather's corpse was robbed by Gaffer.

38. Gold says that Lizzie needs to be cured of her misplaced loyalty to her father, noting "True loyalty is to be oneself." Gold, *Charles Dickens: Radical Moralist*, 259. Gold is right about the change needed in Lizzie, but only in the sense that she needs to be cured of hiding behind this loyalty (not to be cured of the loyalty because her father did not deserve it).

39. Lizzie's goodness is presented first in her uneasiness with her father's occupation and then in her loyalty to him despite her own uneasiness. Her desire to help others, especially Jenny Wren, is further evidence of her goodness.

40. Dyson, *Inimitable Dickens*, 255.

41. Dyson, *Inimitable Dickens*, 255.

42. See chapter 2 of this work for a discussion of Rorty's understanding of personal freedom.

43. As Miller explains, "It is altogether impossible [in *Our Mutual Friend*] to withdraw completely from that situation and to create out of nothing a new self and a new engagement with the world." Miller, *Charles Dickens: The World*, 279–80. Gold also makes this point when he observes that "the presence and power of the past, especially as embodied in parents," require that we come to terms with our past and parents in our quest to discover our true selves. Gold, *Charles Dickens: Radical Moralist*, 258.

44. In commenting on the role of self-definition vis-à-vis faith, Gold puts Dickens's point nicely: "One cannot dig for treasure unless one grants that it may be there. It cannot on the other hand be found without digging." Gold, *Charles Dickens: Radical Moralist*, 278.

45. The Veneerings represent society. For their conferral of identity, see Jennifer Gribble, "Depth and Surface in *Our Mutual Friend*," *Essays in Criticism* 25 (1975): 207.

46. Eugene explains himself to Mortimer, saying "'Anything to carry out M. R. F.'s arrangements, I am sure, with the greatest pleasure—except matrimony. Could I possibly support it? I, so soon bored, so constantly, so fatally?'" (I, 12).

47. Recall his words to Lizzie in which he refers to "'the cursed carelessness that is over-officious in helping me at every other turning of my life.'" (IV, 6).

48. Gribble, "Depth and Surface," 197, drawing on Robert Garis, *The Dickens Theatre* (Oxford: Clarendon Press, 1965), 243.

49. See Gold, *Charles Dickens: Radical Moralist*, 269. Andrew Sanders also points out the significance of Eugene's name, observing that it indicates that he is "well-born." Andrew Sanders, "'Come Back and Be Alive': Living and Dying in *Our Mutual Friend*," *Dickensian* 74 (1978): 140.

50. Self-acceptance involves both self-discovery and an acceptance of one's contingencies, all of the factors that constitute the particularities of one's life. Lizzie and

Eugene have complimentary tasks in the novel: Lizzie must attend to the latter part, while Eugene needs to accomplish the former.

51. Ian Clarke points out that Mortimer means death and sea in "Two Names in *Our Mutual Friend*," *Dickens Studies Newsletter* 14, no. 1 (1983): 13.

52. Jenny's perspicacity is without parallel in the novel and it is required to help Eugene understand what his deep desire is.

53. Margaret Flanders Darby goes so far as to refer to Eugene as "a shadow of a mate" for Lizzie, in "Four Women in *Our Mutual Friend*," *Dickensian* 83, no. 411 (1987): 36.

54. We are told that he was "daily growing stronger and better, and it was declared by the medical attendants that he might not be much disfigured by and by" (IV, 16), and that when he spoke of Lizzie, "The glow that shone upon him . . . so irradiated his features that he looked, for the time, as though he had never been mutilated" (IV, 16).

55. In this sign of peace between him and his father we find an acceptance of the father by the son—an acceptance that speaks to Eugene's acceptance of his initial place in life.

56. Gribble observes that, while John Harmon is the "young man 'feigning to be dead'" who Dickens had mentioned in a note to Forster in 1861, Eugene Wrayburn also fits the bill. See Gribble, "Depth and Surface," 197.

57. Daleski (*Dickens and the Art of Analogy*, 309) and Sanders ("'Come Back,'" 140) are right to call love the regenerative force in the novel. But while love heals and makes new beginnings possible, it does not completely remove the past. Moreover, it is inextricably linked with acceptance, as Miller observes: "The human spirit, in the reciprocity of self-sacrificing love, has the magical power to transform any situation and make any wishes come true, but only through the full acceptance of that situation," though he overstates its regenerative/transformative capacity. Miller, *Charles Dickens: The World*, 327.

58. I agree with Lucas, who says, "For [Dickens] the marriage is redemptive for Eugene, because it frees him from the false and crippling belief that he is a free man [with his social identity]. True freedom turns out to be commitment." Lucas, "In Conclusion," 336. He also suggests that the marriage is as freeing for Lizzie as it is for Eugene (339).

59. Daleski also sees Eugene and Bradley as counterparts, each displaying "alternate possibilities of life in the dust-heap, of life that can be redeemed, Dickens seems to say, only by love." Daleski, *Dickens and the Art of Analogy*, 317. Both Gold and Smith view Rogue Riderhood, a waterside character, as Bradley's true double. Gold, *Charles Dickens: Radical Moralist*, 267; Peter Smith, "The Aestheticist Argument of *Our Mutual Friend*," *Cambridge Quarterly* 18, no. 4 (1989), 379.

60. See Lucas, "In Conclusion," 327, regarding Bradley's desire to have society give him an identity.

61. Even though Lizzie, after rejecting his proposal of marriage, tells him unequivocally that her feelings for him are independent of any "'other living creature,'" Bradley responds by continuing to discuss the centrality of Eugene, not Lizzie or him-

self, in the entire matter. (II, 15). Our sympathy, awakened here by his pathetic obsession, grows as we witness the way that Eugene taunts him with it in III, 10. Of course, Bradley may awaken a strange sympathy, but he does so without ever becoming likable.

62. Of this scene, Lucas observes, "The moment provides one of those great dramatic images which crystallize a theme. It is marvelously apt and it is, of course, terrible. For Bradley's wiping out his name is a final admission that he has not been able to achieve the identity for which he sacrificed his life (literally, as it turns out)." Lucas, "In Conclusion," 329.

63. Bradley also brings about Rogue Riderhood's destruction, of course, when he murders him as part of his own suicide.

64. In its utter lack of giving, it stands in stark contrast to Sydney Carton's self-sacrifice for Charles Darnay at the end of A *Tale of Two Cities*.

65. Dickens presents aspects of his theme in virtually every character of the novel. Such is the richness of his vision that he can successfully treat his theme at once so sweepingly and yet in such minute detail. Obviously, however, space here does not permit a full analysis of this technique, nor of what he has to say with each character.

66. The Boffin plot has a counterpart to Jenny in Mrs. Boffin, for she, too, is accepting and has the ability to see the real identity of others. But it is in Jenny that Dickens most fully brings together the facets of his complex theme.

67. We are told, "It was difficult to guess the age of this strange creature, for her poor figure furnished no clue to it, and her face was at once so young and so old. Twelve, or at the most thirteen, might be near the mark" (II, 1).

68. When asked by Bradley Headstone if she has "'neighbouring children'" to play with, Jenny cries, "'Ah lud! . . . Don't talk of children. I can't bear children. *I* know their tricks and their manners.'" She later adds, "'no, no, no. No children for me. Give me grown-ups'" (II, 1).

69. In II, 2, Jenny tells Eugene and Lizzie of her early and recurring fantasies of fragrant flowers and melodious birds who keep her company.

70. Hence, Lizzie's initial desire to help Jenny, as she puts it to Charley, as a form of "compensation—restitution—never mind the word, you know my meaning. Father's grave" (II, 1).

71. I am referring here to her delicious peppering of Fascination Fledgeby's wounds after his beating at the hands of Alfred Lammle, when Jenny has just come to understand how Fledgeby has compromised her friend Riah. Whether we cheer Jenny on or not is beside the point; Fledgeby has callously wreaked havoc on the lives of numerous characters. The brief suffering she causes him is hardly disproportionate to his offense.

72. G. W. Kennedy sees the assumption of a pseudonym as a conscious act of authority, declaring that it is "the central act of salvation" in the world of *Our Mutual Friend*. G. W. Kennedy, "Naming and Language in *Our Mutual Friend*," *Nineteenth-Century Fiction* 28 (1973): 167–68.

73. Manning, "Modified Satire," 222.

74. Manning notes that, while "her instinct raises her to a sort of supernatural knowing," she is "sharp-tongued." Manning, "Modified Satire," 222.

75. Godmother is her affectionate title for Riah, who is the teacher hired for her and Lizzie by Eugene. Interestingly, Jenny's vision seems to falter for a time regarding Riah. A case could be made, however, that Jenny's uncertainty regarding his character results from her unerring perception, for Riah himself must come to terms with his own complicity in Fledgeby's victimization of him.

76. It is important to distinguish between acceptance and judgment. Jenny could be read as a judgmental character, but that would miss the point of her perspicacity: she sees reality as it is. This does not mean that she likes everything she sees, or that she sugarcoats it. On the contrary, she is as sharp as she is perceptive. The making of judgments is part of how she proceeds in life, as in her assessment that Bradley Headstone is to be avoided.

77. A true rarity in the novel, repeated only in the kindly Mrs. Boffin of the Boffin plot line.

78. Sanders, "'Come Back,'" 136. Manning also reads this as suggesting a limited treatment of death as a release from life. Manning, "Modified Satire," 206.

79. This scene can also be read as Dickens's contemporary version of John 12:25, "Those who love their life lose it, and those who hate their life in this world will keep it for eternal life." *The New Oxford Annotated Bible*, ed. Bruce M. Metzger and Roland E. Murphy, New Revised Standard Version (New York: Oxford University Press, 1991).

80. Daleski says that to die to the world is "to rise above it, to look down on and despise the values of the dust-heap." Daleski, *Dickens and the Art of Analogy*, 289. See also Miller, who sees her remark to Fledgeby as "a kind of final condemnation by Dickens of all those people in his novels who cannot in some way die to the quotidian world and to all its values and conventions." Miller, *Charles Dickens: The World*, 315.

81. Miller links the resurrection to an acceptance of one's original place in the world. It involves this, but only in the sense that it is an acceptance of what one's place was. The accepted self is no longer tied down by the original situation. As Miller explains, this "liberation which allows their former selves to begin again . . . permits a change in orientation from past to future." Miller, *Charles Dickens: The World*, 325.

82. Gold, *Charles Dickens: Radical Moralist*, 276.

83. The very pervasiveness of Dickens's theme of acceptance tells us that he is talking about not just the existence of particular characters, but also about the nature of existence.

84. Although Dickens is not explicitly religious on this point, it is in line with Karl Rahner's assertion that saying "yes" to ourselves is finally how we say "yes" to God, creator of our existence.

85. Of this interconnectedness, Miller comments, "The novel might be seen as a kind of slow dance in which all the possibilities of interaction are displayed one by one." Miller, *Charles Dickens: The World*, 287.

CHAPTER FIVE

An Ethics of Active Acceptance

In part I, the theoretical groundwork was laid for viewing the human person as finite, contingent, and free. The view established there sees human beings in all their vulnerability to finitude and contingency as conditions of existence, yet also recognizes that the human capacity for freedom, to the extent that it exists, complicates this vulnerability, provides a measure of invulnerability, and allows for a fundamental response to these features of existence. In the last chapter of part I, a close reconsideration of the moral luck debate without the assumption of mechanistic determinism that has shaped the debate to date revealed that while we may well have a real capacity for freedom, however circumscribed, and thus not be victims of genuine moral luck, we must exercise our freedom in a world of uneven luck, sometimes hoping to do no more than mitigate tragedy with our freedom.

A desire to understand what this deep but not total vulnerability could mean for our lives led to an examination of Charles Dickens's treatment of vulnerability in *Our Mutual Friend* in the first chapter of part II. Here, Dickens is seen to explore the question in terms of identity. His final word is that we can be effective in the world only when we are able truly to accept the particular self that we are, the one self that is shaped but not wholly determined by the specific contingencies and limitations of our lives. Moreover, by showing the pervasiveness of dependency and limitation in the world of the novel, Dickens suggests that this self-acceptance must include the acceptance of contingency and finitude as conditions of existence. Although he is not explicitly religious on this point, Dickens implicitly points to the religious dimension of self-acceptance by presenting this self-acceptance as encompassing the nature of existence itself. Self-acceptance as a contingent and finite being is thus identified by Dickens as the fundamental moral task, with the suggestion that it has a related religious significance.[1]

It is now time to address the nature of active acceptance and its possibilities for moral discernments about ethical obligation. But before any substantive discussion can begin about acceptance as a moral obligation itself, a move beyond Dickens's treatment is required. In his novel, Dickens demonstrates the need for acceptance, in particular self-acceptance, on essentially practical grounds. Persons can only become efficacious moral actors once they fully accept themselves, the particularities of their lives, and the nature of existence itself. The practical argument supports the insights of part I. Since it is clear that we are contingent and finite to a significant degree at every level of existence, it follows that acceptance of contingency and finitude, including the myriad ramifications these conditions have for our particular lives and the lives of others, will improve our ability to function morally. It makes sense that beings who are deeply vulnerable to these conditions of existence do well to be cognizant and accepting of manifestations of this vulnerability in all of their actions. However, none of these points goes beyond the pragmatic to explain why we might be *obligated* to be accepting in this way. There are two reasons for the difficulty in moving beyond the pragmatic value of acceptance. The first is that acceptance is important in two different respects: as task and as obligation. Because acceptance is a fundamental task that grounds ethical action, and can indeed lead to a methodology for ethical discernment, its practical import comes to the fore. We must look deeper into the conditions of existence in order to see that we are also obligated to be accepting of ourselves and others by the terms of existence itself. The second reason for the difficulty in recognizing acceptance as an ethical obligation is that it is also, at the same time, a religious obligation. Recognition of its religious dimension is important, crucial even, to a full understanding of human obligation generally, but it can make it more difficult for us to see that it is also distinctly ethical. Before turning to the main work of this chapter—an examination of the implications of contingency, finitude, and freedom for understanding how acceptance helps us discern and meet our obligations to one another and ourselves—it is necessary first to explore this religious injunction as it has been understood within the Christian tradition. This is the subject of the first section, in which key aspects of the Christian tradition are identified, which leads into an analysis of self-acceptance as a religious obligation. The final two sections of the chapter focus explicitly on what is proposed as an ethics of acceptance: The second addresses the nature of obligation generally, and acceptance as a particular ethical obligation, one that is profoundly religious, divinely commanded, and also implied in the nature of the fundamental conditions of existence; the third addresses acceptance as an ethical task by outlining a method for discerning the content of specific obligations in terms of active acceptance of self and others, and ultimately of the contingency and finitude of existence.

Religious Obligation and the Christian Tradition

The Christian view of existence emerges directly from its understanding of the story told about Jesus of Nazareth in the New Testament. As William Placher has argued, not uniquely, the story itself is not simply the rendition given by any one evangelist, but rather the meaning that emerges from the New Testament as a whole, and especially from the four gospels.[2] In the various gospels Jesus is depicted with different personality features, different approaches to the concrete problems of existence, and different ways of accepting God's will for him. In this multifaceted depiction itself, then, we have a testimony to the complexity of the contingency and finitude of existence and one person's ultimate response to the demand that existence makes of him. Moreover, just as this story cannot justly bear reduction to one simple account, it also cannot be limited to one form of expression. Its meaning for Christianity can also be told in a variety of nonnarrative ways, one of which is through theological doctrines.

Three interrelated doctrines concerning Jesus are of particular interest here, not so much for the truth they tell us about Jesus, which is their chief aim as theological doctrines, but for the truth they tell us about ourselves. These doctrines are known as the doctrines of incarnation, christology, and soteriology. These doctrines may be stated briefly as follows: The doctrine of incarnation holds that "the Son or Word of God, the second Person of the divine Trinity, assumed a fleshly human body in Jesus Christ and lived a historical existence on this planet, subject to all the constraints and limitations of such an existence."[3] Christology, which presumes incarnation, seeks to explain the nature of Christ. Its classic expression derives from the Council of Chalcedon, in 451 C.E., where it was asserted that "Jesus Christ is one 'person' (the eternal Logos of the Father) in two 'natures' (divine and human)."[4] Modern theologians struggle with how to render this formulation today, but "usually striv[e] to uphold some version of the claim that the personal existence of Jesus as a whole has some kind of unique status and value."[5] Finally, soteriology "embraces two broad areas of theology: the question of how salvation is possible and in particular how it relates to the history of Jesus Christ; and the question of how 'salvation' itself is to be understood."[6]

If we consider these doctrines together, in their broadest strokes, asking not what they say theologically as words about God but what they suggest about human persons, we can say that they bespeak value. The doctrine of the incarnation tells us two things: that God desired a unique and intimate union with humanity[7] and that a human being could "have the capacity for receiving God."[8] Both of these affirmations tell us that we are uniquely valuable: there is something in our nature that is capable of this special kind of relationship with the divine. Christology more specifically affirms that one human being did, in history, receive God in perfect union. Moreover, it depicts God as accepting, in a fundamental way, the conditions of human existence as suitable for divine existence. And soteriology, in its twofold concern with the fact that salvation can be ours and with the nature of salvation, tells us that Jesus accepts even human agony and death for our sake so that we can somehow experience the fullness of our humanity beyond the conditions of existence. We are thus beings of value who are deeply but not wholly vulnerable to the conditions of existence.

A key but unarticulated assumption in all of these doctrines is that Jesus' acceptance of human existence, his acceptance of finitude and contingency, and his willingness to accept even death are all free acts of acceptance of the finitude and contingency of existence. Jesus of Nazareth is a particular, limited, contingent man who faces death by crucifixion at a particular time and place in his own history and in ours. That the Christian tradition also affirms the absolute efficacy of this acceptance in its doctrine of soteriology tells us that acceptance of contingency and finitude in freedom serves a fundamental religious purpose.

When we turn from the Christian story of Jesus' radical and efficacious acceptance to a religious understanding of acceptance for human beings, we see acceptance as a religious obligation. Viewing self-acceptance as a specifically religious obligation is hardly a new or unique idea.[9] As religious beings, we understand ourselves to be called to acceptance. Christians need look no farther than the first commandment to know that we are religiously obligated to love God. Acceptance that includes a deep acceptance of the contingency and finitude of existence is an active affirmation of God's creation of us. As such, it is a loving "Yes," both to ourselves as the created and to the creator, and thus it is a way of fulfilling our obligation to love God. This concept has a special force for Christians, because, as noted above, the Christian tradition is shaped by a story that has radical acceptance at its heart. In Jesus' acceptance of death on the cross, we have before us our preeminent example of radical acceptance of God's will that involves acceptance of the contingency and finitude of the world, so it is no surprise that acceptance figures repeatedly in the way Christians understand their response to the world and, ultimately, to God.[10] Acceptance, and the related ideas of assent to the world and to self, have appeared in the Christian tradition at least since Augustine.[11]

In light of the present project, however, the form of this acceptance can be articulated anew. Since Karl Rahner's anthropology coincides in important respects with the view that emerges from part I, it is not surprising that his thought can serve as a rich resource for this rearticulation. Of course, as noted in chapter 2, his understanding of the transcendent dimension of human persons, particularly in relation to human freedom, does stand in need of a metaphorical reinterpretation. But with such reinterpretation, we are able to benefit from Rahner's clear and profoundly insightful treatment of the religious significance of acceptance.

For Rahner, freedom is both unmediated and mediated. That is, it exists as a transcendental capacity that can only be realized, that is, mediated, in categorical, concrete experience.[12] In general, he accepts the Kantian move to make freedom transcendent, though he does not fully accept Kant's conception of transcendent freedom as metaphysically separable from phenomenal experience. However, Rahner's conception of mediated freedom as supported by a metaphysically transcendent unmediated freedom carries with it an underlying acceptance of Kant's response to Newtonian mechanism. Yet, as was argued in chapter 2, if we no longer assume Newtonian mechanism to be the all-pervasive description of physical existence, then this metaphysical move is not required. Now it is possible to think of freedom as a capacity that stands in relation to and can even be accounted for by the finitude and contingency of existence. When Rahner invokes the concept of transcendental freedom, then, we can cut it free from its metaphysical origin and reinterpret it as referring metaphorically to the ability freedom gives us to transcend, that is, go beyond or not be fully determined by the finitude and contingency of existence. Transcendental freedom as a concept, then, points to the element of noncausality that is expressed as the choosing between multiple possibilities, a coming to be that cannot be accounted for by mechanistic determinism.

With this metaphorical interpretation of transcendental freedom in mind, we can consider what Rahner has to say about acceptance as a religious obligation. For Rahner, the centrality of acceptance can be seen in his insistence that the primary question to be asked in relation to human freedom is, What is this freedom for? Rahner's answer is that acceptance of God and self is freedom's ultimate point. As observed in chapter 2, Rahner is cognizant of our deep vulnerability to the contingency and finitude of existence. Moreover, he helps us see that it is in our actions as finite and historically located persons, in what he calls our categorical experience, that we are able to transcend, that is, go beyond, the conditions of existence as determinative through self-acceptance before God. Our freedom makes this transcendence possible, yet it is an act that can occur only in the concrete actions of life because it is in our categorical experience that we are given opportunities to realize our freedom. Rahner articulates this as a point of unity between categorical and transcendental experience. We can see that unity as occurring because freedom is a feature of existence that allows us to act out of our finite and contingent existence in ways that are not wholly determined by that finitude and contingency. What is important here, though, is that this unity of freedom and the concrete quality of existence illuminates the relationship between the ethical and religious obligation of self-acceptance, for it is only through the actions of our lives that we are able to accomplish the profound, religious act of self-acceptance before God. Rahner's insight that we can use our capacity for freedom to be accepting before God only in the concrete actions of our lives, then, retains its power without the risk of essentializing noted in chapter 2.

Importantly, this link between the ethical and the religious is not sequential but simultaneous. We cannot first say "Yes" to God and ourselves and then engage in the acts of our lives. According to Rahner, it is not possible for us to meet our religious obligation to God apart from the concrete contexts of our lives.[13] Nor is it the case that we can live our lives and then be merely accepted (or rejected) by God. It is helpful to consider Rahner's point that the final outcome of our lives is not an extrinsic moral, juridical decision made about us based on the actions of our lives.[14] It is instead the intrinsic result of our own free act of self-acceptance, for in this "Yes" to our being is ultimately our "Yes" to God.

For Rahner, this is an act that is at once before us, a possibility as a final act, and with us, part of the ongoing activity of life. We can never know if we have genuinely accepted ourselves,[15] so we must live our lives continually striving to accept ourselves. Self-acceptance stands as an ultimate act for us, because at some point it constitutes our final and irreversible decision about our relationship with God. Its finality is what makes it eternally significant: eventually, it stands beyond time, beyond change.[16] However, this eternally significant decision is made only within time. It is achieved through full acceptance of our particular selves with all the details of our lives and our conditions of existence. Our self-acceptance is not a passive acquiescence to all that happens to us. It is instead our own ultimately efficacious acceptance of our "true" selves. This includes acceptance of ourselves as finite and contingent, but also as free, with an obligation to use this freedom to respond to God.

Acceptance and Ethical Obligation

When we accept ourselves and the conditions of our existence, we accept them rather than deny them, but we do not merely resign ourselves to them. Acceptance, then, is not merely a strategy for dealing with vulnerability.[17] Instead, acceptance is a dynamic act that both takes up our past actions and grounds our present actions as we use our freedom creatively to grow and develop. While self-acceptance has an ultimate, religious significance for us, and is indeed a religious obligation for us, the fact that it is accomplished in the concrete moral choices of our lives makes it also an ethical task. Moreover, as Charles Dickens helps us see in *Our Mutual Friend*, self-acceptance is a foundational ethical task, for it is only when we act from a self-accepting stance that we are able to be truly effective in this world. As a ground of our moral actions, it is an act that must be present in some way if our acts are to be morally good. But between religious obligation and ethical task, of which more will be said later, stands the issue of acceptance as a moral obligation. And to explore this issue, we will need also to search for an understanding of the nature of obligation generally.

But first, more can be said concerning the connection between our obligation to love God, an obligation to accept fully ourselves and the conditions of our existence, and acceptance as an ethical obligation. Christian scripture provides the central link. Matthew 22:37–39 reads, Jesus "said to him, 'You shall love the Lord your God with all your heart, and with all your soul, and with all your mind.' This is the greatest and first commandment. And a second is like it: 'You shall love your neighbor as yourself.'" According to Christian interpretation of these love commandments, our obligation to love God is inextricably linked with our ethical obligation to assist others and ourselves.[18] The second commandment is like the first. Given that similarity, fulfillment of the second commandment will be analogous to fulfillment of the first. If, as argued above, acceptance is a fundamental religious obligation that enacts our love of God in our acceptance of our true selves in the concrete actions of our lives, then we can also say that acceptance is a fundamental ethical obligation that makes it possible for us to enact our love of neighbor. We could state the connection even more closely and say that since the obligation to love our neighbor and our self is both a religious and an ethical obligation, acceptance of self and others in ways that recognize the conditions of our existence is a fundamental way in which we fulfill both our religious and ethical obligations.[19] This is not to say, however, that the ethical and the religious collapse into one obligation. The commandment to love neighbor is like the commandment to love God, but it is not identical. There are actions that are uniquely associated with love for God. Prayer and worship, for example, even when they are communally experienced and so may encompass concern for and support for neighbor, are actions undertaken precisely as ways of loving God. Every concrete act of acceptance in its fullest sense, then, is not necessarily also an action that meets both our religious and ethical obligations. While every instance of acceptance that enacts our love of neighbor has a religious significance as well, first because it is a way of meeting a religiously commanded obligation and second because saying "Yes" to ourselves and our neighbor also is saying "Yes" to God, every instance of acceptance is not necessarily directed at meeting our ethical obligation. Some are uniquely religious. It would be a mistake not to see the independent opportunities for responding directly to the commandment to love God in our acceptance of self and particular existence. When we speak, then, of acceptance as an ethical obligation, we understand that this has a religious significance as well, but we do not necessarily imply the converse. Acceptance as an ethical obligation is logically distinct from acceptance as a religious obligation.

Saying that acceptance is a fundamental ethical obligation, however, does not yet tell us about how we are to determine the content of our particular ethical obligations—how it is to function as an ethical task. To move toward that, we need to consider the nature of our ethical obligation to love our neighbors and ourselves. For Christians, it undeniably has the status of a divine command. But because it can be understood in terms of accepting the conditions of existence, it also has a natural standing. That is, the natural and divine command dimensions of the obligation converge, allowing us to consider this obligation in its natural dimension. This is important, because the command to love our neighbor leaves us with many questions as to what this means for us in terms of specific actions in the concrete contexts of our lives. Even though we understand ourselves to be obligated to help others, and even though we have a host of ways in which we are to meet the needs of others, such as the injunctions contained in the Sermon on the Mount,[20] we are often perplexed as to how to respond to our sense of being obligated in particular contexts, to particular persons. Specifying the content of obligations to one another is reserved for the following section, but laying the natural foundation for this task is the goal here. This places the focus on ethical obligation itself.

Once we gain a fuller understanding of obligation in natural terms, that is, obligation itself according the terms of existence, we will be in a better position to think about how this new approach to ethics as acceptance assists in the task of specifying the content of particular obligations.

Discerning Moral Obligation

Before asking how reflections on the conditions of existence can shed light upon the nature of obligation, particularly our obligation to acceptance, it is helpful to recall that a moral obligation of any kind is addressed to a person's freedom. This, of course, is one reason why it was crucial to establish in chapter 2 that the human capacity for freedom cannot be ruled out by science, and that it may even be said that there are scientific grounds for the capacity for freedom. And as we have just seen, freedom is what makes it possible for us to act as finite and contingent beings in ways that meet our obligations. Given the centrality of freedom, we can say that a moral obligation involves something that is being asked of a person, something the person can choose to do or not do. It is also something not only asked of a person but also experienced by the person as a claim. It thus involves the experience that something ought to be done, not merely that something might be good to do. It is not necessary or helpful here to define in detail what differentiates moral obligation from other sorts of obligation (for example, legal obligation), other than to say that moral obligations are those we have toward others or ourselves that are not necessarily enforced by any structure of society. What can be done, however, is to probe in the light of previous considerations some of the relevant bases and dimensions of moral obligation. Reflecting on the conditions of existence can help us make sense of the nature of moral obligation, for it can reveal to us how this obligation fits in as a part of human existence as a whole and show us how acceptance of the conditions of existence is a crucial, one could say primary or foundational, ethical obligation.

Without claiming to construct a comprehensive analysis or method for describing the contours of moral obligation in natural terms, it is possible to indicate some of the important insights or clues for discernment of moral obligation generally and, in particular, the obligation of acceptance that the consideration of human beings as finite, contingent, and free generates. Five insights in particular seem immediately recognizable. The first one is that we are obligated according to the terms of existence itself. The fact that human existence is limited and dependent means that we can exist only through our dependency on others and in our own limited ways. Our sheer existence, experienced in this way, suggests an obligation to let others depend upon us just as we inescapably depend on others. This goes deeper than surface or recip-rocal interdependencies; it goes beyond simply sustaining a social fabric, as important as this is. We do not just depend on others for this or that—we *are*, in our being, dependent. We do not just experience some limitations that give rise to need—we *are*, essentially, limited. We do not, then, merely incur specific debts to individuals and society that can be repaid simply by re-sponding to a few specific needs of others.

We can see this better if we start with what we have come to see as a fun-damental moral task: self-acceptance. Acceptance of ourselves as deeply but not utterly vulnerable to contingency and finitude forms a starting point for understanding the nature of obligation because it is also our first obligation to ourselves. Indeed, if we recall that the command to love neighbor instructs us to love our neighbor as ourselves, then we can recognize the appropriate-ness of looking at acceptance of ourselves to understanding the nature of our obligation to others. When we accept ourselves, we accept that we are deeply dependent and limited beings—beings, in fact, who exist through contin-gency and finitude. This entails accepting the particular dependencies and limitations that characterize our own lives. But in accepting this about our-selves, we are accepting, perhaps unreflectively, that such is the nature of ex-istence. I would not be the me that I am were it not for the unique ways that contingency and finitude have shaped my life, which include the way that these conditions have also shaped the lives of those around me. Gradually, if I continue to think along these lines, I see the expansion of the roles of con-tingency and finitude in shaping lives to the point where I recognize their roles in shaping all life. The conclusion that particular existence occurs by and through contingency and finitude is inescapable.[21]

Once I admit that contingency (dependency) and finitude (limitation) obtain at the heart of existence—that we could not exist as we are without them—then I have to reckon with the roles that radical dependency and limitation play in life. I begin to see that however unique a being I may be, I am not wholly responsible for who I am, what I do, and what I do not do. My very uniqueness is dependent upon and limited by a seemingly infinite num-ber of factors and occurrences. As I see how I am affected by others, be it my parents who gave me my genetic makeup or the driver who will signal prop-erly on the highway later today and thus not cause me to be in a fatal acci-dent, I see the ways in which I have the potential to affect others. If I am consistent in my reflections, I cannot avoid recognizing that I exist in a ma-trix of contingency and finitude, affected by and affecting others.

This recognition leads me, indeed, obligates me, to accept that there is an interconnectedness to life that is deeper than mere surface interdependencies. Interdependencies that exist on the surface of life give rise to a way of understanding obligation reciprocally. While this is a valuable understanding, it is vulnerable on two sides. On one hand, claims that I am obligated to help another who depends on me because in some other way I depend on this person may be valid, but fail to move me to meet my obligations, because I can argue that I am willing to forgo any subsequent benefit to me (or even society) that might result from any act of assistance on my part. On the other hand, if I do find such claims persuasive such that I am moved to meet my obligations, I might feel unable to resist the claims of others on me, to the point where I am consumed by feelings of duty.[22] I may thus meet many obligations toward others but fail to meet any toward myself.

A fuller understanding emerges from the consideration of life, that is, particular existence, as contingent and finite, and so deeply interconnected, because now I view my obligations as arising not just from some historical fact, such as that a particular person needs my assistance, but from the fact that none of us exists without experiencing deep limitation in herself and radical dependency on others. When I experience myself as obligated to help another, I need to understand that meeting this obligation is a way of responding to the need of a particular person and *also* to the nature of human existence. That I am in a position to help another is not solely to my credit, and that the other needs my help is not to that person's debit. Instead, it is part of the structure of existence that we all sometimes need assistance and sometimes are capable of providing assistance, because the contingency and finitude of existence create both the need and potential for help in all of us.

A second and closely related insight is that meeting our obligations to one another and ourselves is a primary way in which we actualize our self-acceptance.[23] The reciprocal of this was noted above in connection with understanding how acceptance helps us fulfill the divine command to love neighbor. But here we see it in terms of the nature of existence, because self-acceptance involves an acceptance of the conditions of existence. To accept ourselves fully, we must accept that we are all finite and contingent, that we exist through contingency and finitude. When we are willing to meet our obligations to others, whether this means the provision of assistance to another, the nurturing of the young and the weak, or the keeping of commitments to one another and ourselves, we are accepting and affirming ourselves as contingent and finite beings who participate in this contingent and finite life. Attempts to ignore our true obligations are rejections of ourselves and the nature of our existence. Conversely, accepting our obligations is the way that we actualize our self-acceptance, and self-acceptance that includes acceptance of the conditions of existence enables us to meet our obligations to others. This means that we must both accept and be accepting. We must accept the conditions of existence, and we must be accepting of particular needs and capacities that arise universally from the conditions of existence.

A third insight concerning obligation emerges from the Christian view of the human person as deeply but not utterly vulnerable to the conditions of our existence. As beings who are more than what happens to them, as beings who have the capacity to act in freedom to decide about ourselves in a way that has eternal significance, we are beings with an enduring value.[24] This makes what happens to us all the more significant. Our vulnerability is a vulnerability that matters. Thus, the obligations we have to ourselves and others are not mere opportunities to go through the motions of contingent existence, but the chance to help and care for beings of value. We can see the significance if we compare the view of the human person that was established in part I, a view that is compatible with key Christian doctrines that bespeak intrinsic human value, with the notion of human responsibilities that Richard Rorty's account might suggest. Recalling from chapter 2, in Rorty's view we are completely contingent, with no question of enduring value. Rorty is willing to identify only the capacity for humiliation as a common and distinctly human characteristic, because humiliation is the one form of suffering unique to human beings. Rorty maintains that it is good to relieve suffering, but he cannot generate a moral obligation to relieve suffering, even humiliation, on the basis of any human capacity, for two reasons: first, because our solidarity extends only to those we wish to include in the category of persons, not necessarily to every human being who suffers humiliation, and second, because he has given up on the possibility of our private convictions (including philosophical ones) giving rise to public obligations. Rorty can give good reasons for meeting the needs of others, and he clearly hopes that we will do so, but his philosophical position prevents him from going beyond good reasons to obligation. But even if he could generate an obligation, he would be at a loss to explain why we would feel moved to meet the obligation toward beings who had no intrinsic value. He would allow that we can bestow value on those whom we consider human persons, but that does not entail that we feel morally obligated to be open to claims for acceptance and care from those not so designated. His view has the effect, potentially at least, of artificially limiting the moral claims that can be made on each of us. But if intrinsic human value is part of our understanding of what it is to be a human being, then we must respect that the value itself places a moral claim on us.

The fourth insight that these considerations yield is that if contingency and finitude characterize our existence, then they also characterize the nature of obligation. Obligations themselves are contingent and finite, existing in an intricate web of dependency and limitation. Our obligations are contingent: they arise from the particular dependencies of life, as well as from the particular capacities of individuals to meet them. Every person is not obligated to help every other person at all times. We have specific obligations to specific people at specific times, as they do to us, based upon individual relationships, needs, and capacities. The existence of need can place a claim on us, if we have the capacity to help, and if the need is not relativized by another's need. The intricacy of the web of existence resulting from the contingency of existence thus tells us two things: first, that sometimes people do depend upon us and have a claim on us and, second, that we have the corresponding potential to affect some people at some junctures in life. But needs and claims require comparative adjudication; we are not obligated beyond our capacity to help.

Similarly, the finitude that characterizes obligations also tells us that they are limited.[25] We are not obligated, nor are we able, to provide any kind of absolute assistance to another human being. Obligations end. Moreover, obligations can be met by others than ourselves. Sometimes, even if we have the capacity to help someone, it is up to us to let another person provide the assistance. We are not just respecting our own limits when we sometimes say "No" to another in need. We are instead recognizing that there is someone else who is in a more appropriate position to help, even if we could somehow be of assistance.

If we consider that obligations are both contingent and finite, then we also recognize that our obligations are less cut and dried than we would like them to be, as are others' obligations to us. There are times when it is obvious that another is truly dependent upon us for help. An infant in our care is radically dependent upon us for meeting her immediate needs, and there is no ambiguity about this dependency. But often our obligations are clothed in uncertainty. We may not know if another is genuinely dependent upon us (much less what that dependency might entail). If we are to understand obligations, our understanding must encompass our inability to remove all uncertainty traceable to our own limitations and the intricacy of the web of interdependence that characterizes all existence.

Yet another, a fifth, insight is that if we are all deeply vulnerable to the conditions of existence, and thus all limited and dependent in significant respects, we are in no position to be condemning others for their limitations and dependencies. Contingency and finitude are shared and inescapable features of existence. Recognizing this tempers our impulse to judge others. As emphasized in chapter 3, there is a difference between discernment and judgmentalism. Certainly, we must engage in discernment when we make moral choices. To do otherwise is to act without responsibility to ourselves and others. However, a convenient way to evade awareness that an obligation has a claim upon *us* is to judge *another* as somehow uniquely responsible for every facet of her or his own limitation and need. Such a judgment distances us from our sense of interconnection and mistakenly absolves us from our obligation to the one judged. It amounts to a denial of the conditions of existence and is thus a way of rejecting those conditions and ultimately our own true selves.

These five insights help us understand the nature of obligation as qualified and constituted by the contingency and finitude of existence. They also help us understand acceptance as a natural obligation. While acceptance as an obligation arises explicitly from the first two insights, we can see that the last three also point toward an obligation to accept the contingency and finitude, not just of existence generally, but of particular persons, ourselves included. Existence itself obligates us to assist particular others and to accept that obligation resides in the structure of existence. This, in turn, not only converges with the divine command to love our neighbors as ourselves, but also gives us a way of determining particular obligations. The insights arising from a consideration of human beings as finite, contingent, and free are clues for understanding the nature of ethical obligation, but more than that. Once in place, they serve as necessary presuppositions for all of our moral deliberations, because they establish our natural obligations to acceptance of the conditions of existence for its own sake and as a way of meeting obligations to ourselves and others. Yet, as here articulated, they remain formal. As such, they press us to a further concern for specification of the content of our obligations.

Acceptance as an Ethical Task:
Specifying the Content of Our Obligations

As we move to explore ways in which knowledge of the conditions of existence and our vulnerability to them help specify the content of our obligations to ourselves and others, whether we consider that obligation under its divine or natural status, we must bear in mind an aspect of the fourth insight into the nature of obligation suggested above: obligation is characterized by uncertainty. We need a way of identifying *when* we are obligated and *what* it is we are obligated to do, but we must undertake this moral discernment with the cautions of acknowledged ambiguity. There is no safe way to live, no absolutely clear-cut path through our moral lives.

Of course there is a range in the degree of uncertainty associated with discernment of our obligations to another or to self. In part, this is because there is a range of kinds of obligations to one another and ourselves. Obligations are endemic to the structure of our existence, but not all particular obligations are already given in the structure of our own existence. That is to say, our strongest and most identifiable obligations are often ones we ourselves initiate and undertake. These are obligations that arise out of the commitments we make, whether explicitly or implicitly. Having a child, for example, contains an implicit commitment to care for that child. A parent does not have to cast about trying to identify whether or not she is obligated to the child for care. The obligation is clear. However, even here, it is not always obvious what the obligation entails in specific circumstances and at specific times. The required needs of an infant, for example, for love and nourishment and protection from the elements, are fairly easy to ascertain (though even here, there can be uncertainty). As the child grows, the content of the obligation changes. At some point, the parent may even become obligated not to provide food and shelter, or not to provide it without the child's contribution. Even when we know clearly that a specific form of obligation endures, we may still not know so clearly what it requires of us at particular times.

In another example, we recognize an explicit commitment to another in marriage or partnership or community involves new obligations to the other. Here, again, it is easy to identify that an obligation exists, but the specific requirements of the commitment, or the way in which one is obligated to meet them, may change. Indeed, the relationship may change so dramatically that the obligation to the other holds only in the way that it is severed.[26] So even in the cases in which we place ourselves in a position of obligation toward another, how we are to fulfill that obligation, and in some cases if we are to fulfill it in any way connected with how we are expected to meet it, is still a matter surrounded by uncertainty.

Yet we cannot allow this uncertainty to prevent us from attempting to act in ways that meet our ethical obligations. Moreover, this uncertainty exists alongside the practical implication of what it is we accept when we accept the conditions of our existence. As beings who exist in and through finitude and contingency, but with freedom and hence the capacity for self-acceptance and for responding to God, we act in accordance with our nature when we are accepting of ourselves and others as finite, contingent, and free. But we accept not just in this general sense. What we need to be aware of specifically are the particular ways each of us is limited and dependent in particular contexts of life. If we can be aware in this way, then we can see not just that we are in fact obligated in terms of the conditions of existence itself, but that acceptance as a specific ethical task helps us identify how it is we are to meet our obligations. What is yielded by the considerations of contingency and finitude, of vulnerability, and of the nature of obligation broadly understood are three questions that help us identify the content of our obligations.

Questions for Specific Discernment

While we have seen that we have an ethical obligation to accept the conditions of existence, it has also become apparent that acceptance itself is a fundamental ethical task that makes it possible for us to identify and meet our specific obligations. In turning from consideration of ethical obligation generally to specific obligation, the first question that should be asked is: *What is most self-accepting?* As noted in an earlier section, it is fitting to begin with self-acceptance, because we can move from what we understand about our need to accept ourselves to a deeper understanding of what acceptance of all of existence involves. But more than this is at stake. If we are not first accepting of ourselves, then we are not yet in a position to be accepting of others and able to meet their needs. Self-acceptance is a practical prerequisite for moral action.

In *Our Mutual Friend*, Charles Dickens shows us how asking what is most self-accepting translates into the activity of ordinary human life by making us see that it is genuine self-acceptance that grounds our moral action and allows us to be truly effective in the world. As we have seen, it is only after Lizzie Hexam is willing to accept herself fully, including her past share in the activity of her father, that she is able to help Eugene Wrayburn. Her self-acceptance frees her so that she is able to admit her own love for Eugene and meet the obligations that engenders, as he lay healing from Bradley Headstone's attack. If Lizzie had not accepted this past, she would simply not have been able to rescue Eugene. Instead, she would have failed to meet her obligations both to save the drowning man and to open herself to the man she loved. This example also brings to life the point that our self-acceptance, however necessary to ground moral action, does not happen in a vacuum. It happens in the midst of life. Lizzie, it is true, does flee London, but not for a solitary, self-accepting experience. She flees it to protect herself. When she finally achieves full self-acceptance, she is prompted to do so by the need of another, a drowning man. We accept ourselves in helping others;[27] we find ourselves in finding our place in the network of existence.

Not surprisingly, it is possible for us to use supposed obligations to others as a way of avoiding self-acceptance. In another novel, *Bleak House*, Dickens gives us the example of a certain Mrs. Jellyby who spends her entire life "helping" people a continent away while utterly neglecting her own children. Dickens describes her in his cast of characters as "a lady devoted to public duties, to the neglect of her home."[28] She suffers from a kind of moral myopia, seeing the need only of others at a great distance. When any of us fall into a similar myopia, it reflects a denial of ourselves, of our particularities, which include the dependencies that stand in immediate relation to us. Accepting ourselves involves an acceptance of our particular situation with its particular claims upon us.[29]

We must also consider our own specific limitations and capacities when answering the question, What is most self-accepting? If we simply do not have the talents or the resources needed to help another, we are not obligated to provide them. Obligation, it must be remembered, is addressed to our freedom. We must be able to choose to meet the obligation. That means that the choice must be of an option that is real.[30] Or, as Kant put it, "Ought implies can." If our self-acceptance is realistic, then it will be an acceptance of who we are, with our own actual talents and capacities. We cannot take on obligations that we only wish we could meet, nor should we ignore obligations we are well suited to meet. Our task is to determine whether meeting a particular obligation truly includes accepting ourselves.

Finally, when asking what is most self-accepting in attempting to determine when and how we are obligated to ourselves and others, we need to consider what is most accepting of our "true" selves, who we feel ourselves really and uniquely to be. This implies the inevitability of our own struggles to find our true selves. In *Our Mutual Friend*, Eugene's first task is to discover himself. He cannot possibly see how he might be obligated to Lizzie in love until he can see who he is himself. As we saw in chapter 4, self-acceptance involves more than a mere resignation to the particular dependencies and limitations of our lives. Instead, it requires that we accept the particularities of our lives for what they are, and move from that point to grow and develop creatively. We cannot be obligated to do things that would prevent us from acting out of our true selves. Eugene, for example, has a duty to respect his father, but he is not obligated to marry someone just because his father wishes him to marry.

Likewise, there are obligations that stand before us that have the possibility of helping us to grow and develop as we truly are. Marrying Lizzie is just such an obligation for Eugene, as marrying Eugene is for *Lizzie*. For these two characters, full growth is possible only when they actualize that part of their identity that is to be realized as the spouse of the other. Failing to see that such an obligation applies to oneself is a denial of one's true self, or a refusal to see one's true self, both of which are ways of avoiding self-acceptance.

Sometimes, accepting ourselves involves, as it does for Eugene, that we struggle with and let go of patterns of existence that inhibit our growth. It can also require that we seek to cast off cruelty and oppressiveness that others inflict upon us. In Jenny Wren, Dickens gives us someone who must attempt to contain the abusiveness and harm of her situation, even though she cannot free herself of it entirely. Her assumption of the role of parent in relation to her father illustrates her taking charge of him and controlling the deleterious effects of his behavior on her life to the extent that she is able. Likewise, her accepting Lizzie's and Riah's friendship and care demonstrates her willingness to be protected from the harm that is part of the givenness of her situation.

A second question arises from the third insight concerning the nature of obligation, that we are beings of value. If no person is merely the sum of what happens to her or him, and if each person has the possibility of relating to God in a final way, then no person is without unique and enduring value. When we ask the question, *What is accepting of human value?* we focus our attention on the value of human beings, both ourselves and possible recipients. When we are aware of someone's need that we might be in a position to meet, we must evaluate our ability and desire to help in light of this value. Moreover, we need to remember that at times the contingency of existence means that we actually are in a position where someone depends upon us, uniquely us, for assistance and that we are in fact in a position to supply this assistance. Respecting this value means that we will recognize that we have the obligation and will decide to meet it. Attempts to dehumanize and disregard human value provide rationalizations for avoiding the strength of others' claims on us, but they are false precisely insofar as they avoid full acceptance of the reality of human existence. What we must accept is that life is structured such that beings of value sometimes have needs and we sometimes have capacities to help others, and vice versa. Deciding whether or not an obligation exists must take this into consideration. Even when we discern that we are not the appropriate person to provide assistance in a particular case, we must not dismiss the value of the one we do not help. To do otherwise is to deny the reality of existence and thus to fail in our task of a full self-acceptance that includes acceptance of existence.

Nor can we forget, as we seek to discern specific obligations toward others, that we also are beings of value. Asking, What is accepting of human value? requires us to assess our own value in determining our obligations to others. Even in the face of another's great need or dependency on us, we are not morally obligated to meet that need, serve that dependency, if doing so destroys or compromises our own value, our own dignity as human beings. We might even be in a position where we feel obligated to risk our lives for another, but not our value. For example, when Lizzie swims to rescue Eugene, she puts herself at risk without knowing who is in danger. It might be Bradley Headstone instead of Eugene. Taking a personal risk for one in so grave a need is all that matters. Earlier, though, she clearly has no obligation to sacrifice her dignity to satisfy Bradley's need to have her in his life. Neither does she have any obligation to sacrifice her dignity to accept Eugene on dishonorable terms before he has the courage to embrace his own identity and respect her value. Accepting that others depend on us and that they have value does not mean that we can satisfy them at a cost of denying our own human value.

A third question that is helpful in specifying the content of an obligation once we have identified that an obligation exists asks: *Is this way of meeting the obligation conducive to the recipient's own self-acceptance?* Our actions toward others must respect that every other person also needs to be self-accepting. If our doing a deed of love for another inhibits the other's own ability to accept herself, then that deed is an inappropriate way for us to meet the obligation. The obvious way in which this can be harmful to another is by unnecessarily increasing her dependency on another and thereby creating an unrealistic sense of vulnerability. It is true to the conditions of human existence to recognize that we are all dependent upon others, and that sometimes individuals are dependent upon us in particular ways, as we are upon others. It is not true to existence, however, to gain an advantage over another by creating an undo dependency on us. This is the kind of dependency that Bradley wants to create for Lizzie. He wants to "lift" her out of her circumstances in order to make her forever grateful to him. It is also the way that he treats Charley Hexam, Lizzie's younger brother, whom he is grooming to be a schoolmaster like himself.

It is less obvious but also possible to meet an obligation to another such that we mask their true dependency, and this also does not respect their own need to see and accept themselves as they are. If we care for a child to the extent that he or she grows up unaware of the real work involved in caring for oneself—taking responsibility for one's choices, maintaining one's home and clothing, preparing one's food, earning one's livelihood, and so on—we may create an unrealistic sense of independence and invulnerability. Our care masks the reality of life for the child, so that the child enters adulthood unaware of the real and demanding work of life. The obligation to care thus is met improperly, because it is done in such a way as to inhibit the child's ability to accept herself and the particularities of life realistically.

When we ask if a particular way of meeting an obligation is conducive to the recipient's own self-acceptance, we are also asking whether or not it allows the recipient to recognize and accept her own finitude. We need to be aware, when we are attempting to discern the content of an obligation to another, whether or not what we do for that person either exaggerates or minimizes the recipient's real limitations. If we meet the obligation to feed hungry persons in a way that unduly emphasizes their poverty and their inability to provide for themselves, we are providing them with an exaggerated conception of their limitation. For example, if we respond to a person's particular need for food without also indicating ways we know of that the person might acquire her own food (through a food cooperative, for example), we are making her feel more limited in her ability to provide for herself than she truly is.

But the question also reminds us that we cannot meet our obligations to others in a way that seeks to transcend the recipient's real limitations. If we pay for a child to attend college, for example, when the child does not have the academic ability or skills necessary to succeed, we are not meeting our obligation appropriately. It may even be the case that the child manages to graduate from college, but is ill-equipped to perform at the level expected of a college graduate. In the process, a false sense of ability and entitlement might be engendered in the recipient, so that a whole new set of limitations are created.

What may be the most difficult discernment of all with respect to limitation is the decision whether what we are attempting to do for another will push back limitations appropriately or deny them. There are times when we may be poised to help another move past a real limitation; we should not confuse such opportunities with the denial of limitations. Medical situations in which a person is limited by illness or a physical condition come readily to mind. If we are in a position to help another or ourselves receive healing or therapeutic treatment, then we should do so. However, what is appropriately healing for one person may amount to a denial of limitation for another, and we need to be aware of this difference. For example, resuscitating a person in an accident situation may be obligatory, while resuscitating a person who is actively dying (that is, literally and inevitably dying) is contrary to one's obligation. Accepting life as it is means accepting that sometimes we must help another push back limits, but not in such a way that denies the real and concrete limitation of particular existence.

Finally, asking, Is this way of meeting the obligation conducive to the recipient's own self-acceptance? requires us to consider what self-acceptance might entail *for* the recipient. It requires, in other words, attention to what Gene Outka calls recipient autonomy. Yet, since it asks not specifically what the recipient wants but what is conducive to the recipient's own self-acceptance, some protection is provided against allowing a recipient's wants to become tyrants to our own moral senses.[31] Likewise, this question insists that we not make the recipient a victim of our own wants and desires. When we are deciding what our obligations to another are, there is an appropriate focus on our actions, but it must not be so narrow as not to include in its view the recipient's own obligation to self-acceptance as a being who is finite, contingent, and free.

These three questions, taken together, do not form a blueprint for moral discernment that will lead inexorably to particular conclusions regarding moral obligations. Particular individuals will disagree, for example, on whether or not an action that pushes back limitations does so in a way that is accepting of the conditions of existence. Advances in medical technology are likely candidates for disagreement, for example. Yet this inability to generate unambiguous specifications as to the existence of a moral obligation and what it entails is not a weakness but a strength of this approach. Because we are all deeply vulnerable beings, uniquely shaped by the particular contingencies and limitations of our own existence and our own use of our freedom, we need an ethical approach that allows us to work with our particularity to help us move toward identification of our obligations to others who are as uniquely shaped as ourselves. This respect for particularity does not equate with a full-blown moral relativism. No claim is being made that obligations are not real, or that others cannot have claims on us that challenge us to rethink our values or to respond out of a sense of duty. We need to discern when and how we are obligated, but we do not get to choose relative to our preferences. What this ethics of acceptance asks of us is not easy; it does not involve merely identification of particular preferences. It asks us to discern our genuine obligations, no matter how difficult it may be to meet them. But it does move away from having as its goal the assignment of moral responsibility for morally good or bad, or right or wrong, actions. It instead seeks to determine what is most accepting of the conditions of existence for particular human beings. In this shift, we have a move toward viewing the ethical choices each of us encounters in life, not as isolated moments in an historically unified existence, but as parts of an integrated approach to life. This means that we may be able to discover coherent approaches to some of the most troubling ethical questions we face. The coherence is gained by always asking, in each moment, what is most accepting in the broad, active, and dynamic sense outlined here. If this method succeeds in helping us identify and understand our obligations as interconnected and arising from the structure of existence, then its ethical yield will be substantial. Even more, if in the process of using acceptance as a way of discerning particular ethical obligations we also work toward meeting our general religious obligation to God, then we will see how our ethical choices all form part of the fabric of our response as creatures to creation and to creator. This is fitting for the kinds of beings that we are: finite, contingent, and free, grounded by and oriented toward mystery.

Notes

1. Dickens's treatment of self-acceptance points to the religious significance, even though it focuses on the ethical task. The religious significance of his treatment of identity in *Our Mutual Friend* has been well documented. For example, see Karen Hattaway's "Entering into the Kingdom: Charles Dickens and the Search for Spiritual Regeneration" (Ph.D. diss., Rice University, 1981).

2. William C. Placher, *Narratives of a Vulnerable God: Christ, Theology, and Scripture* (Louisville, Ky.: Knox, 1994), 88. Placher himself quotes Paul Ricoeur in support of this view.

3. John Macquarrie, "Incarnation," in *The Blackwell Encyclopedia of Modern Christian Thought*, ed. Alister McGrath (Cambridge, Mass.: Blackwell, 1993).

4. Bruce D. Marshall, "Christology," in *Blackwell Encyclopedia*.

5. Marshall, "Christology."

6. Alister McGrath, "Soteriology," in *Blackwell Encyclopedia*.

7. For example, see Karl Barth's description of the significance of Emmanuel, "God with Us," in *Church Dogmatics*, Vol. 4, bk. 1, trans. G. W. Bromiley (Edinburgh: T. & T. Clark, 1956), 3–21.

8. Macquarrie, "Incarnation." This latter meaning is also clear to Karl Rahner. Anne Carr states, "Thus the human person can be understood as the possibility of incarnation, as the possible material for God's own history." Anne Carr, *The Theological Method of Karl Rahner* (Missoula, Mont.: Scholars, 1977), 138.

9. Psychological and philosophical renderings of this idea exist that take account of the task as a religious one. For an example of a psychological rendering, see Ernest Becker's final chapter in *The Birth and Death of Meaning: An Interdisciplinary Perspective on the Problem of Man* (New York: Free Press, 1971), especially pages 194–99. Paul Ricoeur uses the idea philosophically (as consent), but with a religious thrust, to reconcile the persistent question of freedom versus physical determination in *Freedom and Nature: The Voluntary and the Involuntary*, trans. Erazim V. Kohák (Evanston,

Ill.: Northwestern University Press, 1966). See also John Haught, *Religion and Self-Acceptance* (New York: Paulist, 1976) for an articulation of the philosophical dimensions of this religious task.

10. Of course, Christianity is not univocal on this point. Reformed theology, for example, would insist that obedience is the fundamental response required of human persons. However, full, active acceptance of the conditions of existence can be translated into a language of obedience, albeit with a different accent, so the two views are not necessarily incompatible.

11. Augustine says, "To yield our consent, indeed, to God's summons, or to withhold it, is (as I have said) the function of our own will." Augustine, "A Treatise on the Spirit and the Letter," in *Nicene and Post-Nicene Fathers of the Christian Church*, vol. 5, *Saint Augustin: Anti-Pelagian Writings*, ed. Philip Schaff, trans. Benjamin B. Warfield (Grand Rapids, Mich.: Eerdmans, 1978), chap. 60, xxxiv.

12. For Rahner, the categorical experience is concrete experience that occurs in history, as distinguished from transcendental experience.

13. Rahner follows Aquinas closely here, with his understanding of the simultaneity of material and formal willing, and the need for good material acts to will God formally so that they are a way of "the soul turn[ing] to God." See *Summa Theologica*, I–II, 19, 10 and I, 93, 8.

14. Rahner, *Foundations*, 39.

15. Rahner does allow for one possible exception in *On Prayer*, where he refers to the case in which a person has "confirmation in grace." See *On Prayer* (Collegeville, Minn.: Liturgical, 1993), 85–86.

16. That it be final and eternally valid requires us to be finite, even if there had been no Fall. For Rahner, death is required by our nature as free beings who have the possibility of a free and irreversible decision about ourselves. See "On Christian Dying," *Theological Investigations, Vol. 7*, trans. David Bourke (New York: Herder and Herder, 1971), 286–89.

17. See the end of chapter 1, where denial and resignation were noted as strategies for dealing with vulnerability.

18. This is not an uncontroversial interpretation of the love commandments. For an account of the issues and an endorsement of the view that the command includes an injunction not only to neighbor love but also to self love, see Gene Outka, "Universal Love and Impartiality," in *The Love Commandments*, ed. Edmund Santurri and William Werpehowski (Washington, D.C.: Georgetown University Press, 1992), 5–10.

19. Rahner sees the connection as one of union. While the object of the love of God is higher than that of love of neighbor, fulfillment of each one ultimately and simultaneously encompasses the other. Karl Rahner, "Reflections on the Unity of the Love of Neighbour and the Love of God," *Theological Investigations Vol. VI*, trans. Karl-H. Kruger and Boniface Kruger (New York: Seabury, 1974), 231–49.

20. Matthew 6–7; Luke 6:17–49 (Sermon on the Plain).

21. Note that the conclusion obtains for particular existence, not existence *per se*.

22. This problem plagues utilitarianism, and is known as the problem of negative responsibility. See Bernard Williams' account in J. J. Smart and Bernard Williams, *Utilitarianism: For and Against* (New York: Cambridge University Press, 1973), 95.

23. Compare this with Rahner's idea that we say "Yes" to God in the concrete actions of our lives.

24. This way of putting it is primarily Rahner's, but the assertion that we are beings of enduring value is implied in the Christian doctrines of the incarnation and salvation.

25. For a theological reflection on this topic, see Gilbert Meilaender, *The Limits of Love: Some Theological Explorations* (University Park: Pennsylvania State University Press, 1987), 16–17.

26. For an account of the possibilities giving rise to a desire to be released from this kind of commitment, see Farley, *Personal Commitments: Beginning, Keeping, and Changing* (San Francisco: Harper and Row, 1986), 73–79.

27. Rahner also points to the role of self-acceptance in meeting the needs of the neighbor in "The 'Commandment' of Love in Relation to the Other Commandments," in *Theological Investigations*, Vol. V, trans. Karl-H. Kruger (New York: Crossroad, 1966). Rahner asserts, "Morality is the free personal acceptance of one's own pre-established nature, confidently coming to grips with one's own dynamic reality in all its united though multiple dimensions and precisely coming to grips also with that nature which realizes itself only when it turns lovingly to another person and when it accepts its own nature as the nature of the mystery of love" (441).

28. Charles Dickens, *Bleak House* (New York: Holt, Rinehart and Winston, 1970), xxxv. See also chapter IV of the novel, "Telescopic Philanthropy."

29. This is not to deny that we can have obligations to those who are distant from us. It is merely to say that we cannot use efforts to meet those obligations as excuses to neglect the needs of those more immediately dependent upon us.

30. For a description of the elements of free choice, see Farley, *Personal Commitments*, 25–29.

31. The concern for the risk of tyranny is also Gene Outka's.

Select Bibliography

Allison, Henry E. *Kant's Theory of Freedom*. New York: Cambridge University Press, 1990.

Andre, Judith. "Nagel, Williams, and Moral Luck." In *Moral Luck*, edited by Daniel Statman, 123–29. Albany: State University of New York Press, 1993.

Aquinas, Thomas. *Summa Theologica*. Translated by the Fathers of the English Dominican Province. Westminster, Md.: Christian Classics, 1948.

Arendt, Hannah. *The Human Condition*. Chicago: University of Chicago Press, 1958.

Augustine. "On the Spirit and the Letter." In *Nicene and Post-Nicene Fathers of the Christian Church*, edited by Philip Schaff. Vol. 5, *Saint Augustin: Anti-Pelagian Writings*. Revised Translation by Benjamin B. Warfield. Grand Rapids, Mich.: Eerdmans, 1978.

Barth, Karl. *Church Dogmatics*. Vol. 4, bk. 1. Translated by G. W. Bromiley. Edinburgh: T. & T. Clark, 1956.

Becker, Ernest. *The Birth and Death of Meaning: An Interdisciplinary Perspective on the Problem of Man*. New York: Free Press, 1971.

———. *The Denial of Death*. New York: Free Press, 1973.

———. *The Revolution in Psychiatry*. New York: Free Press, 1964.

Bentham, Jeremy. *Principles of Morals and Legislation*. London: Clarendon Press, 1907.

Bresnahan, James F. "An Ethics of Faith." In *A World of Grace*, edited by Leo J. O'Donovan, 169–84. New York: Crossroad, 1989.

Browne, Brynmor. "A Solution to the Problem of Moral Luck." *Philosophical Quarterly* 42, no. 168 (1992): 345–56.

Calvin, John. *Institutes of the Christian Religion*. Edited by John T. McNeill, translated by Ford Lewis Battles. 2 vols. Library of Christian Classics, vol. 21. Philadelphia: Westminster, 1960.

Card, Claudia. *The Unnatural Lottery: Character and Moral Luck*. Philadelphia: Temple University Press, 1966.

Carr, Anne. "Starting with the Human." In *A World of Grace*, edited by Leo J. O'Donovan, 17–30. New York: Crossroad, 1989.

———. *The Theological Method of Karl Rahner*. Missoula, Mont.: Scholars, 1977.

Clarke, Ian. "Two Names in *Our Mutual Friend*." *Dickens Studies Newsletter* 14, no. 1 (1983): 12–14.

Cotsell, Michael. *The Companion to "Our Mutual Friend."* Boston: Allen & Unwin, 1986.

D'Arcy, Eric. *Human Acts: An Essay in Their Moral Evaluation*. Oxford: Oxford University Press, 1963.

Daleski, H. M. *Dickens and the Art of Analogy*. London: Faber and Faber, 1970.

Darby, Margaret Flanders. "Four Women in *Our Mutual Friend*." *Dickensian* 83, no. 411 (1987): 24–39.

Davies, Paul. *The Mind of God: The Scientific Basis for a Rational World*. New York: Simon & Schuster, 1992.

———. "Physics and the Mind of God: The Templeton Prize Address." *First Things* 55 (1995): 31–35.

Dickens, Charles. *Bleak House*. Introduction and notes by Albert J. Guerard. New York: Holt, Rinehart and Winston, 1970.

———. *Great Expectations*. New York: Washington Square, 1956.

———. *Hard Times*. New York: Harper Classic, 1968.

———. *Little Dorrit*. Edited by John Holloway. Baltimore: Penguin, 1967.

———. *Oliver Twist*. Afterword by Edward Le Comte. New York: Signet Classics, 1961.

———. *Our Mutual Friend*. New York: Bantam, 1990.

———. *A Tale of Two Cities*. Introduction by Edgar Johnson. New York: Washington Square, 1939.

Dictionary of Religion and Philosophy. S.v. "Contingency." Edited by Geddes MacGregor. New York: Paragon House, 1989.

Dobrin, David N. "A Note on Jenny Wren's Name." *Dickens Studies Newsletter* 9 (1978): 48–49.

Dyson, A. E. *The Inimitable Dickens*. New York: St. Martin's, 1970.

Edwards, Paul, ed. *Encyclopedia of Philosophy*. New York: Macmillan, Free Press, 1967. S.v. "Contingent and Necessary Statements," by D. W. Hamlyn. S.v. "Logic, Modal," by A. N. Prior.

Erhueh, Anthony O. *Vatican II: Image of God in Man*. Rome: Urbaniana University Press, 1987.

Farley, Margaret. *Personal Commitments: Beginning, Keeping, Changing*. San Francisco: Harper and Row, 1986.

———. "The Role of Experience in Moral Discernment." In *Christian Ethics: Problems and Prospects*, edited by Lisa Sowle Cahill and James F. Childress, 134–51. Cleveland: Pilgrim, 1996.

Feinberg, Joel. "Equal Punishment for Failed Attempts: Some Bad but Instructive Arguments against It." *Arizona Law Review* 37 (1995): 117–33.

Frankfort, Harry. *The Importance of What We Care about: Philosophical Essays*. New York: Cambridge University Press, 1988.

Gold, Joseph. *Charles Dickens: Radical Moralist*. Minneapolis: University of Minnesota Press, 1972.

Gould, Stephen Jay. "Humbled by the Genome's Mysteries." *New York Times on the Web*, February 19, 2001, Opinion section.

Greenstein, Michael. "Mutuality in *Our Mutual Friend*." *Dickens Quarterly* 8, no. 3 (1991): 127–34.

Gribble, Jennifer. "Depth and Surface in *Our Mutual Friend*." *Essays in Criticism*, 25 (1975): 197–214.

Guerard, Albert J. Afterword to *Bleak House*, by Charles Dickens. Introduction and notes by Albert J. Guerard. New York: Holt, Rinehart and Winston, 1970.

Gustafson, James. *Ethics from a Theocentric Perspective. Vol. 1: Theology and Ethics*. Chicago: University of Chicago Press, 1981.

Hall, David. *Richard Rorty: Prophet and Poet of the New Pragmatism*. Albany: State University of New York Press, 1994.

Hardy, Barbara. *The Moral Art of Dickens*. New York: Oxford University Press, 1970.

Harvey, Anthony, ed. *God Incarnate: Story and Belief*. London: SPCK, Holy Trinity Church, 1981.

Hattaway, Karen Ann Kennett. "Entering into the Kingdom: Charles Dickens and the Search for Spiritual Regeneration." Ph.D. diss., Rice University, 1981.

Haught, John F. *Religion and Self-Acceptance*. New York: Paulist, 1976.

Hecimovich, Gregg. "The Cup and the Lip and the Riddle of *Our Mutual Friend*." *English Literary History* 62 (1995): 955–77.

Hegel, Georg W. F. *Hegel's Philosophy of Right*. Translated by T. M. Knox. New York: Oxford University Press, 1967.

Hirsch, Gordon D. "Psychological Patterns in the Double Plot of *Our Mutual Friend*." *University of Hartford Studies in Literature* 12, no. 3 (1980): 195–221.

Hollis, Martin. "The Poetics of Personhood." In *Reading Rorty: Critical Responses to "Philosophy and the Mirror of Nature" (and Beyond)*, edited by Alan Malachowski, 244–56. Cambridge, Mass.: Blackwell, 1990.

Hornback, Bert G., and Joel J. Brattin. *"Our Mutual Friend": An Annotated Bibliography*. New York: Garland, 1984.

Horne, Lewis. "*Our Mutual Friend* and the Test of Worthiness." *Dalhousie Review* 62, no. 2 (1982): 292–302.

House, Humphry. *The Dickens World*. 2d ed. New York: Oxford University Press, 1960.

Jackson, Timothy. "The Disconsolation of Theology." *Journal of Religious Ethics* 20, no. 1 (Spring 1992): 1–35.

———. "The Theory and Practice of Discomfort: Richard Rorty and Pragmatism." *Thomist* 51, no. 2 (1987): 270–98.

Janssens, Louis. "Ontic and Moral Evil." In *Readings in Moral Theology No. 1: Moral Norms and Catholic Tradition*, edited by Charles E. Curran and Richard A. McCormick, 40–93. New York: Paulist, 1979.

Jensen, Henning. "Morality and Luck." In *Moral Luck*, edited by Daniel Statman, 131–40. Albany: State University of New York Press, 1993.

Johnson, Edgar. *Charles Dickens: His Tragedy and Triumph*. 2 vols. New York: Simon & Schuster, 1952.

Kant, Immanuel. *Critique of Practical Reason*. Translated by Lewis White Beck. New York: Macmillan, 1956.

———. *Groundwork of the Metaphysic of Morals*. Translated by H. J. Paton. New York: Harper and Row, 1964.

———. "On a Supposed Right to Lie from Altruistic Motives." In *Moral Absolutism*, edited by Joram Graf Haber, 15–19. Lanham, Md.: Rowman & Littlefield, 1994.

———. *Prolegomena to Any Future Metaphysics*. Revised Paul Carus translation. Indianapolis: Bobbs-Merrill, 1950.

Karakunkel, George. *The Christian Vision of Man*. Bangalore, India: Asian Trading Corporation, 1984.

Kennedy, G. W. "Naming and Language in *Our Mutual Friend*." *Nineteenth-Century Fiction* 28 (1973): 165–78.

Kenny, Anthony. "Aristotle on Moral Luck." In *Modern Thinkers and Ancient Thinkers*, edited by Robert. W. Sharples, 157–71. London: University College London Press, 1993.

Kierkegaard, Søren. *Sickness Unto Death*. Translated by Walter Lowrie. Princeton, N.J.: Princeton University Press, 1954.

Knauer, Peter. "The Hermeneutic Function of the Principle of Double Effect." In *Readings in Moral Theology No. 1: Moral Norms and Catholic Tradition*, edited by Charles E. Curran and Richard A. McCormick, 1–39. New York: Paulist, 1979.

Lauritzen, Paul. "Hear No Evil, See No Evil, Think No Evil: Ethics and the Appeal to Experience." *Hypatia* 12, no. 2 (Spring 1997): 83–104.

———. "Philosophy of Religion and the Mirror of Nature: Rorty's Challenge to Analytic Philosophy of Religion." *International Journal for Philosophy of Religion* 16 (1984): 29–39.

Levi, Don S. "What's Luck Got to Do with It?" In *Moral Luck*, edited by Daniel Statman, 109–21. Albany: State University of New York Press, 1993.

Lieberman, Daniel E. "Upending the Expectations of Science." *New York Times on the Web*, July 14, 2002, Opinion section.

Lucas, John. "In Conclusion: *Our Mutual Friend*." In *The Melancholy Man*. London: Methuen, 1970.

Luther, Martin. *Martin Luther: Selections from His Writings*. Edited and with an introduction by John Dillenberger. New York: Anchor, 1961.

Lynch, William. *Images of Hope*. Baltimore: Helicon, 1965.

MacIntyre, Alasdair. *After Virtue: A Study in Moral Theory*. Notre Dame, Ind.: University of Notre Dame Press, 1984.

————. *Dependent Rational Animals: Why Human Beings Need the Virtues*. Chicago: Open Court, 1999.

Manning, Sylvia Bank. Epilogue to *Dickens as Satirist*. New Haven, Conn.: Yale University Press, 1971.

————. "Modified Satire: *Our Mutual Friend*." In *Dickens as Satirist*. New Haven, Conn.: Yale University Press, 1971.

McCarthy, Thomas. "Ironist Theory as a Vocation: A Response to Rorty's Reply." *Critical Inquiry* 16, no. 3 (Spring 1990): 644–55.

————. "Private Irony and Public Decency: Richard Rorty's New Pragmatism." *Critical Inquiry* 16, no. 2 (Winter 1990): 355–70.

McClure, Joyce Kloc. "The Contingency of Solidarity: A Pragmatic Critique of Richard Rorty's Philosophy." *Horizons* 28, no. 1 (Spring 2001): 30–49.

McGrath, Alister E., ed. *The Blackwell Encyclopedia of Modern Christian Thought*. Cambridge, Mass.: Blackwell, 1993. S.v. "Incarnation," by John Macquarrie. S.v. "Christology," by Bruce D. Marshall. S.v. "Soteriology," by Alister E. McGrath.

Meilaender, Gilbert. *The Limits of Love: Some Theological Explorations*. University Park: Pennsylvania State University Press, 1987.

Miller, J. Hillis. *Charles Dickens: The World of His Novels*. Bloomington: Indiana University Press, 1969.

Modras, Ronald. "Implications of Rahner's Anthropology for Fundamental Moral Theology." *Horizons* 12, no. 1 (1985): 70–90.

Mooney, Christopher F. *Theology and Scientific Knowledge*. Notre Dame, Ind.: University of Notre Dame Press, 1996.

Nagel, Thomas. "Freedom." In *The View from Nowhere*. New York: Oxford University Press, 1986.

————. "Moral Luck." In *Mortal Questions*. New York: Cambridge University Press, 1978.

————. "Subjective and Objective." In *Mortal Questions*. New York: Cambridge University Press, 1978.

————. "What Is It Like to Be a Bat?" In *Mortal Questions*. New York: Cambridge University Press, 1978.

The New Oxford Annotated Bible. Edited by Bruce M. Metzger and Roland E. Murphy. New Revised Standard Version. New York: Oxford University Press, 1991.

Niebuhr, Reinhold. *The Nature and Destiny of Man: A Christian Interpretation*. Vol. I. New York: Charles Scribner's Sons, 1964.

Nussbaum, Martha C. *The Fragility of Goodness: Luck and Ethics in Greek Tragedy and Philosophy*. New York: Cambridge University Press, 1986.

————. *Love's Knowledge: Essays on Philosophy and Literature*. New York: Oxford University Press, 1990.

Nussbaum, Martha C., and Jonathan Glover, eds. *Women, Culture, and Development*. Oxford: Clarendon Press, 1995.

O'Donovan, Leo J. "A Journey into Time: The Legacy of Karl Rahner's Last Years." *Theological Studies* 46 (1985): 621–46.

————, ed. *A World of Grace: An Introduction to the Themes and Foundations of Karl Rahner's Theology.* New York: Crossroad, 1989.

O'Donovan, Oliver. "Intention." In *Peace and Certainty: A Theological Essay on Deterrence.* Grand Rapids, Mich.: Eerdmans, 1989.

Outka, Gene. *Agape: An Ethical Analysis.* New Haven, Conn.: Yale University Press, 1972.

————. "Universal Love and Impartiality." In *The Love Commandments,* edited by Edmund Santurri and William Werpehowski, 1–103. Washington, D.C.: Georgetown University Press, 1992.

The Oxford English Dictionary. 2d ed. New York: Oxford University Press, 1989. S.v. "vulnerability" and "vulnerable."

Peters, Ivars. *The Mathematical Tourist: Snapshots of Modern Mathematics.* New York: W. H. Freeman, 1988.

Placher, William C. *Narratives of a Vulnerable God: Christ, Theology, and Scripture.* Louisville, Ky.: Knox, 1994.

Plato. *The Republic of Plato.* Translated by Allan Bloom. New York: Basic, 1968.

Rahner, Karl. "Anonymous Christian." In *Theological Investigations,* vol. 6. Translated by Karl-H. Kruger and Boniface Kruger. New York: Seabury, 1974.

————. "The 'Commandment' of Love in Relation to the Other Commandments." In *Theological Investigations,* vol. 5. Translated by Karl-H. Kruger. New York: Crossroad, 1966.

————. "The Dignity and Freedom of Man." In *Theological Investigations,* vol. 2. Translated by Karl-H. Kruger. New York: Crossroad, 1963.

————. "The Experiment with Man." In *Theological Investigations,* vol. 9. Translated by Graham Harrison. New York: Herder and Herder, 1972.

————. *Foundations of Christian Faith: An Introduction to the Idea of Christianity.* Translated by William V. Dych. New York: Crossroad, 1978.

————. "Ideas for a Theology of Death." In *Theological Investigations,* vol. 13. Translated by David Bourke. New York: Crossroad, 1975.

————. "On Christian Dying." In *Theological Investigations,* vol. 7. Translated by David Bourke. New York: Herder and Herder, 1971.

————. *On Prayer.* Collegeville, Minn.: Liturgical, 1993.

————. "On the Question of a Formal Existential Ethics." In *Theological Investigations,* vol. 2. Translated by Karl-H. Kruger. New York: Crossroad, 1963.

————. "The Quest for Approaches Leading to an Understanding of the Mystery of the God-Man Jesus." In *Theological Investigations,* vol. 13. Translated by David Bourke. New York: Crossroad, 1975.

————. "Reflections on the Unity of the Love of Neighbour and the Love of God." In *Theological Investigations,* vol. 6. Translated by Karl-H. Kruger and Boniface Kruger. New York: Seabury, 1974.

————. "Theology of Freedom." In *Theological Investigations,* vol. 6. Translated by Karl-H. Kruger and Boniface Kruger. New York: Seabury, 1974.

Rawls, John. *A Theory of Justice.* Cambridge, Mass.: Belknap, 1971.

Rescher, Nicholas. "Moral Luck." In *Moral Luck*, edited by Daniel Statman, 141–66. Albany: State University of New York Press, 1993.

Richards, Norvin. "Luck and Desert." In *Moral Luck*, edited by Daniel Statman, 167–80. Albany: State University of New York Press, 1993.

Ricoeur, Paul. *Fallible Man*. Translated by Charles Kelbley. Chicago: Henry Regnery, 1965.

———. *Freedom and Nature: The Voluntary and the Involuntary*. Translated by Erazim V. Kohák. Evanston, Ill.: Northwestern University Press, 1966.

Rist, J. M. *Stoic Philosophy*. New York: Cambridge University Press, 1969.

Rorty, Richard. *Achieving Our Country: Leftist Thought in Twentieth-Century America*. Cambridge, Mass.: Harvard University Press, 1998.

———. *Consequences of Pragmatism*. Minneapolis: University of Minnesota Press, 1982.

———. *Contingency, Irony, and Solidarity*. New York: Cambridge University Press, 1989.

———. *Essays on Heidegger and Others*. New York: Cambridge University Press, 1991.

———. "Feminism and Pragmatism." In *The Tanner Lectures on Human Values*, vol. 13, edited by Grethe B. Peterson, 3–35. Salt Lake City: University of Utah Press, 1992.

———. "Inquiry as Recontextualization." In *The Interpretive Turn*, edited by David R. Hiley, James F. Bohman, and Richard Shusterman, 59–80. Ithaca, N.Y.: Cornell University Press, 1991.

———. *Objectivity, Relativism, and Truth*. New York: Cambridge University Press, 1991.

———. *Philosophy and the Mirror of Nature*. Princeton, N.J.: Princeton University Press, 1979.

Ryan, Alan, ed. Introduction to *Utilitarianism and Other Essays: J. S. Mill and Jeremy Bentham*, by J. S. Mill and Jeremy Bentham. New York: Penguin 1987.

Sanders, Andrew. "'Come Back and Be Alive': Living and Dying in *Our Mutual Friend*." *Dickensian* 74 (1978): 131–43.

Shakespeare, William. Sonnet XII. *The Complete Works of William Shakespeare*. Edited by Hardin Craig and David Bevington. Glenview, Ill.: Scott, Foresman, 1951.

Smart, J. J. C., and Bernard Williams. *Utilitarianism: For and Against*. New York: Cambridge University Press, 1973.

Smith, Peter. "The Aestheticist Argument of *Our Mutual Friend*." *Cambridge Quarterly* 18, no. 4 (1989): 363–82.

Spiegel, Murray R. *Schaum's Outline of Theory and Problems of Statistics*. New York: McGraw-Hill, 1961.

Spiegelberg, Herbert. *The Phenomenological Movement*. Boston: Martinus Nijhoff, 1982.

Statman, Daniel. Introduction to *Moral Luck*, edited by Daniel Statman, 1–34. Albany: State University of New York Press, 1993.

Stout, Jeffrey. *The Flight from Authority: Religion, Morality, and the Quest for Autonomy*. Notre Dame, Ind.: University of Notre Dame Press, 1981.

Taylor, Charles. "The Dialogical Self." In *The Interpretive Turn: Philosophy, Science, Culture*, edited by David R. Hiley, James F. Bohman, and Richard Shusterman, 301–14. Ithaca, N.Y.: Cornell University Press, 1991.

———. "The Diversity of Goods." In *Philosophy and the Human Sciences: Philosophical Papers 2*. New York: Cambridge University Press, 1985.

———. "Rorty in the Epistemological Tradition." In *Reading Rorty: Critical Responses to "Philosophy and the Mirror of Nature" (and Beyond)*, edited by Alan Malachowski, 257–75. Cambridge, Mass.: Blackwell, 1990.

———. "Self-Interpreting Animals." In *Human Agency and Language: Philosophical Papers 1*. New York: Cambridge University Press, 1985.

———. *Sources of the Self: The Making of the Modern Identity*. Cambridge, Mass.: Harvard University Press, 1989.

Thomson, Judith Jarvis. "Morality and Bad Luck." In *Moral Luck*, edited by Daniel Statman, 195–215. Albany: State University of New York Press, 1993.

Tillich, Paul. *The Courage to Be*. New Haven, Conn.: Yale University Press, 1952.

Walder, Dennis. *Dickens and Religion* Boston: Allen & Unwin, 1981.

Walker, Margaret Urban. "Moral Luck and the Virtues of Impure Agency." In *Moral Luck*, edited Daniel Statman, 235–50. Albany: State University of New York Press, 1993.

Williams, Bernard. "Ethical Consistency." In *Problems of the Self: Philosophical Papers 1956– 1972*. New York: Cambridge University Press, 1973.

———. "Moral Luck." In *Moral Luck: Philosophical Papers 1973–1980*. New York: Cambridge University Press, 1981.

———. "Persons, Character and Morality." In *Moral Luck: Philosophical Papers 1973–1980*. New York: Cambridge University Press, 1981.

———. Postscript to *Moral Luck*. Edited by Daniel Statman, 251–58. Albany: State University of New York Press, 1993.

Wilson, Edmund. "Dickens: The Two Scrooges." In *The Wound and The Bow*. Boston: Houghton Mifflin, 1941.

Winslow, Joan D. "The Number Plans for Our Mutual Friend: A Note." *Dickens Studies Newsletter* 9 (1978): 106–8.

Wright, Fred A., et al. "A Draft Annotation and Overview of the Human Genome." *Genome Biology* 2, no. 7 (July 2001): 0025.1–0025.18.

Zimmerman, Michael J. "Luck and Moral Responsibility." In *Moral Luck*, edited by Daniel Statman, 217–33. Albany: State University of New York Press, 1993.

Index

About the Author

Joyce Kloc McClure is assistant professor of religion at Oberlin College where she teaches in the field of religious social ethics. A graduate of the College of the Holy Cross, she completed her doctoral studies at Yale University.